Hintergrund

55

Impressum / Imprint

Herausgeber*innen / Editors:
Angelika Fitz, Katharina Ritter, Architekturzentrum Wien
Redaktion / Project Editing: Sonja Pisarik
Buchgestaltung / Graphic Design: Thomas Kussin, buero8
Lektorat / Proofreading: Brigitte Ott (D), Joshua Korn (E)
Übersetzungen / Translations: Susanne Watzek, Judith Wolfframm

Dieser *Hintergrund* erscheint anlässlich der Ausstellung
„Assemble. Wie wir bauen" (01.06. – 11.09.2017), Architekturzentrum Wien.
This *Hintergrund* was published on the occasion of the exhibition
"Assemble. How we build" (01.06. – 11.09.2017), Architekturzentrum Wien.

Kuratorinnen der Ausstellung / Curators of the exhibition: Angelika Fitz, Katharina Ritter
Ausstellungskonzept und -gestaltung / Exhibition concept and design: Assemble
Ausstellungsgrafik / Graphic design: Fraser Muggeridge studio

Bildnachweis / Photo credits:
© Assemble (soweit nicht anders angegeben / unless otherwise stated)

Dank an / Thanks to:
TU Wien / future.lab und Institut für Kunst und Gestaltung / David Calas
RD Foundation Vienna
Bundesministerium für Verkehr, Innovation und Technologie / Stadt der Zukunft
Wienerberger Ziegelindustrie GmbH
British Council

Cover: Detailaufnahme Yardhouse, Fassade / Detail Yardhouse, Facade

Druck / Print: Holzhausen Druck GmbH, Wolkersdorf

ISBN 978-3-03860-077-0

© 2017 Architekturzentrum Wien und Park Books, Zürich

Architekturzentrum Wien, Museumsplatz 1, A-1070 Wien
t +43 1 522 31 15, f +43 1 522 31 17
office@azw.at
www.azw.at

HOW WE BUILD
ASSEMBLE
WIE WIR BAUEN

Angelika Fitz, Katharina Ritter, Architekturzentrum Wien (Ed./Hg.)

AzW Architekturzentrum Wien  PARK BOOKS

Assemble
assembling the Yardhouse
Assemble beim
Aufbau des Yardhouse

Content *Inhalt*

ANGELIKA FITZ
Introduction 08
                                      ANGELIKA FITZ
                               16 Einleitung

OLIVER WAINWRIGHT   OLIVER WAINWRIGHT
Snapshots of the possible 22 Momentaufnahmen des Möglichen

- 40 The Cineroleum
- 46 Sugarhouse Studios
- 52 Yardhouse
- 60 Blackhorse Workshop
- 68 OTOProjects
- 74 Granby Four Streets
- 84 Granby Workshop
- 90 Granby Winter Garden
- 96 Baltic Street Adventure Playground
- 104 Goldsmiths Art Gallery

MARIA LISOGORSKAYA, LEWIS JONES
How we build. Assemble visiting 110
professorship at the TU Wien   MARIA LISOGORSKAYA, LEWIS JONES
                             114 Wie wir bauen. Assembles
                                    Gastprofessur an der TU Wien

NIAMH RIORDAN   NIAMH RIORDAN
The Stucco Paradox 126 Das Stuck-Paradox

INTERVIEW WITH GERHARD ZSUTTY   INTERVIEW MIT GERHARD ZSUTTY
Vienna grew out from its 144 Wien ist aus seinem eigenen
own Underground   Untergrund herausgewachsen

Entrance
Sugarhouse Studios, 2016
Eingang Sugarhouse Studios, 2016
© Angelika Fitz

Introduction "Assemble brought the Turner Prize to the people's living room", to quote the succinct comment of one resident of Granby Four Streets when we visited the project there in the summer of 2016. It was hard to imagine beforehand that this prestigious distinction – probably the most important European art award, after all – would emerge from the everyday reality of a working-class district in Liverpool. The exact focus of the prize is a trifle hard to pin down: is it about the urban renewal plan or the mantelpieces made of recycling material, the communal greenhouse or the newly established social enterprise? Is it about the various alliances with the surrounding neighbourhood or the door handles smoked in a domestic barbecue, the handmade tiles or the generous spatial atmosphere that greets the visitor inside these rather modest-looking terraced houses?

Assemble engage in a unique blend of social activation and collaborative production, poetic spaces and ecological and economic sustainability. Their projects are prototypes of how a society might rethink the way it approaches building. How we build, how things are made and how materials are assembled reveal the very state of a society – this is the consequential conviction of Assemble. The art of this London-based collective lies in transforming the status quo through collaborative action. Time and again, I have been impressed and intrigued by the daring of their projects and the visionary nature of their decisions over the last few years. Already their first undertaking, the Cineroleum, involving the transforma-

tion of a derelict petrol station into a temporary cinema, went far beyond the traditional aesthetic codes of the maker movement. This was a marriage of low-tech manufacture and atmospheric luxury, low-budget materials and detailed sophistication. It must have been an unforgettable experience when, at the end of a film, the fabric walls were raised to reveal a view of the city, when the last images of the film and the visuals of everyday street life overlapped briefly before the eyes of the audience.

In 2010, the Cineroleum project marked the founding and mission of Assemble. Self-organised collaborative action, self-initiated projects, a hands-on approach to building and operating – these were the practices that brought the 18 members of the collective together, already then in its current form, shortly after their graduation from architecture and other disciplines at Cambridge University. A short time later they created affordable creative workspaces and a cultural landmark with Yardhouse and the first of several social enterprises in their young career with the Blackhorse Workshop. Another example is Granby Workshop, part of the Granby Four Streets project, where Assemble work together with the residents' Community Land Trust to revive and transform a traditional working-class neighbourhood in Liverpool in architectural, social, and economic terms. It is not only in the context of Granby Workshop that Assemble engage in astounding experiments with materials. When building the performance and workshop space OTOProjects, they incorporated rubble found on the premises and transformed it into sturdy walls with

excellent acoustic properties. For the facade of the Goldsmiths Art Gallery they are currently experimenting with transforming fibre-cement panels, investing them with unparalleled glamour. The quantum leap in scale of this most recent project and the related question as to how this new dimension will impact the collective's approach would have been reason enough to organise the world's first overview exhibition of Assemble and their work. But why did I decide to begin my tenure as Director of Architekturzentrum Wien with this exhibition?

Since I took up office, I have actually been asked several times whether I was going to devise a programme for an architecture museum that would also be interesting for non-architects. Has architecture divorced itself from everyday life to such a degree? Does society no longer expect anything from architecture? I for one refuse to believe that and have therefore put the question "What can architecture do?" at the centre of our new programme. The "can do" part relates first and foremost to reclaiming the capability to act. In recent years, many architects have developed a feeling of impotency: the construction industry complex seems all too powerful, the system too over-regulated and many decision-makers too disinterested in quality and building culture. Assemble have made it their goal to become empowered again. Imbued with an explicit – yet pragmatic – sense of optimism, they are working to achieve a shift from investor-driven to user-driven architecture and urban development. This includes new formats for co-authorship, co-production and new alliances beyond the confines of the architectural communities.

"Can do" also implies the required skills and know-how. What can a material do? What can form do? It is impressive to see, for instance, how just a few architectural interventions have created an atmosphere at Blackhorse Workshop that goes far beyond customary gender policies and familiar approaches. In fact, when visiting the site I noticed a striking number of women at work. What can solidarity do? Since the 1960s, we have seen the trend to set up collectives come and go in waves. At times they appeared more like rock stars, at others more like smart, diversified start-ups. From the outset, Assemble were not only concerned with their own collective, but intended also to forge alliances with other groups, such as the Community Land Trust in Liverpool. "Assemble are architects", commented a local activist, who "hear and see the voices, dreams and capabilities of others". It is this complex skillset that produces poetically charged, socially diverse and resilient architecture.

"What can architecture do?" also means asking what could be imaginable and feasible. The question opens up a speculative relationship with reality. What, for instance, might architecture look like if children are involved in the planning? Since verbal communication turned out to be inadequate for having a real say – in this as in other participatory endeavours – children from 6 to 12 years of age are supported to self-organise and co-build at the Baltic Street Adventure Playground. "Better a broken bone than a broken spirit" is the leitmotif of Assemble's adventure playground where the children continue to co-design both, their relations and their

built environment on a daily basis. Waterproof clothing and welly boots are provided.

The exhibition *Assemble. How we build* at Architekturzentrum Wien will enable visitors to experience ten selected projects in a very direct way in large-scale installations. Videos, drawings, and other types of documentation will explain the collaborative processes involved in assembling their projects. Sample materials add a haptic level of experience. This publication in the Az W series *Hintergrund* provides an echo and gives those unable to attend the exhibition a first taste of the work of Assemble. The publication will also include material from a one-year visiting professorship of Assemble in Vienna. From the very first discussions in preparation for the exhibition, I considered it important not only to document their work, but also bring Assemble's way of working to Vienna. This wish was fulfilled through co-operation with the Faculty of Architecture and Planning of the Vienna University of Technology. Together with students and David Calas as the local teacher, Assemble asked the question: "How does Vienna build?" An intense architectural investigation of the historical materiality of the city placed the focus on brick and its social, economic, and ecological contexts. In their second term, the students became a maker's collective: how might Vienna build? In a collaborative design process they developed a pavilion for the courtyard of Architekturzentrum Wien. An experiment using bricks and clay, the structure is to be built by the students themselves. The pavilion with its integrated kiln will turn into a workshop in summer for new pro-

duction experiments and classes. When this publication appears, the construction of the pavilion will still be in progress. It was deliberately scheduled to last three weeks beyond the opening of the exhibition. The collective construction process thus becomes part of the exhibition. The pavilion is not only a public workshop but also an inviting, airy venue at the MQ during the summer, a site of collective reflection on what architecture can contribute to a good life.

Hence, the question "What can architecture do?" has also turned into "What can an architecture exhibition do?" My thanks go to all collaborators who were ready to engage in this adventure. I am particularly grateful to Assemble, especially Maria Lisogorskaya and Lewis Jones, for their intense and inspiring collaboration; thanks must also go to the Vienna University of Technology, particularly Dean Rudolf Scheuvens and the Dean of Studies Christian Kühn, as well as future.lab and the knowledge platform Öffentlicher Raum established in co-operation with the City of Vienna, the Institute of Arts and Design, David Calas and all the students. Thanks also go to Wienerberger Ziegelindustrie GmbH and especially Vanessa Rausch for their support as well as to CREAU, Lukas Böckle for the use of their workshops. I am greatly indebted to my co-curator Katharina Ritter, the authors of this publication, to Sonja Pisarik for the editing and the entire team of Architekturzentrum Wien, with whom co-production day-to-day is a genuine pleasure.

Angelika Fitz, Vienna, March 2017

Assemble is a multi-disciplinary collective working across architecture, urbanism and art.
Assemble arbeiten als multidisziplinäres Kollektiv grenzüberschreitend zwischen
den Feldern von Architektur, Urbanismus und Kunst. © Harry Borden

Einleitung "Assemble brought the Turner Prize to the people's living room", so das trockene Fazit einer Bewohnerin von Granby Four Streets bei unserem Besuch im Sommer 2016. Bis dahin war es schwer vorstellbar, dass eine derart hochdekorierte Würdigung – es geht hier immerhin um den wohl wichtigsten europäischen Kunstpreis – mit dem Alltag eines Liverpooler Arbeiterviertels verknüpft wird. Dabei ist das ausgezeichnete Werk in diesem Fall nicht so eindeutig greifbar: Ist es der urbanistische Sanierungsplan oder der aus Recyclingmaterialien gefertigte Kaminsims, der gemeinschaftliche Wintergarten oder das neu gegründete Sozialunternehmen? Sind es die vielfältigen Allianzen mit der Nachbarschaft oder die im Kugelgrill gebrannten Türgriffe, die handgemachten Fliesen oder die großzügigen Raumgefüge, die beim Eintritt in die eher bescheidenen Reihenhäuser überraschen?

Assemble verbinden in ihrer architektonischen Arbeit in einzigartiger Weise soziale Aktivierung und Koproduktion, poetische Räume sowie ökologische und ökonomische Nachhaltigkeit. Ihre Projekte sind Prototypen dafür, wie eine Gesellschaft anders bauen könnte. Wie wir bauen, wie die Dinge gemacht sind und wie Materialien zusammengefügt werden, an diesen Verhältnissen zeigt sich der Zustand einer Gesellschaft, so der weitreichende Befund von Assemble. In der Veränderung des Status quo durch gemeinschaftliches Handeln liegt die Kunst des Londoner Kollektivs. Der Wagemut in ihren Aktionen und ihrer weitreichenden Entscheidungen haben mich in den letzten Jahren immer wieder beeindruckt und überzeugt. Schon ihr Erstlingswerk, das Cineroleum, ein im Selbstbau errichtetes temporäres Kino in einer aufgelassenen Tankstelle, ging weit über die

bekannten ästhetischen Codes der Do-it-together-Bewegung hinaus. Lowtech und atmosphärischer Luxus, Low-Budget und detailgetriebene Raffinesse reichen sich die Hand. Unvergesslich muss der Augenblick gewesen sein, wenn am Ende einer Vorstellung die textilen Wände nach oben gerafft wurden und der Panoramablick auf die Stadt frei geworden ist, wenn sich die letzten Filmbilder und das Straßenleben kurz auf der Hornhaut überlagert haben.

Das Cineroleum markiert im Jahr 2010 den Gründungsimpuls von Assemble. Im selbstorganisierten gemeinsamen Tun, in der Selbstbeauftragung, im Selberbauen und Selberbetreiben fand das Kollektiv, kurz nach Abschluss der unterschiedlichen Studien der 18 Mitglieder, an der Universität Cambridge zusammen, und das bereits in seiner heutigen Form. Kurze Zeit später schufen sie mit dem Yardhouse leistbare Ateliers und eine kulturelle Landmark sowie mit dem Blackhorse Workshop eines von mehreren Sozialunternehmen in ihrer jungen Karriere. Eines davon ist der Granby Workshop als Teil des Projekts Granby Four Streets, wo mit dem lokalen Community Land Trust an der architektonischen, sozialen und ökonomischen Wiederaneignung eines historischen Arbeiterviertels in Liverpool gearbeitet wird. Nicht nur im Granby Workshop schaffen Assemble immer wieder Materialexperimente, bei denen man sich die Augen reiben muss. So wurde beim Konzert- und Proberaum OTOProjects am Gelände vorgefundener Bauschutt zu tragenden Wänden mit hervorragenden akustischen Eigenschaften verarbeitet, und für die Fassade der Goldsmiths Art Gallery werden gerade Faserzementplatten in 1:1-Experimenten verfremdet und mit einem bisher unbekannten Glamourfaktor versehen. Der mit dem zuletzt genannten

Projekt anstehende Maßstabssprung und die damit einhergehende Frage, wie sich dieser auf die Praxis des Kollektivs auswirken wird, wären schon Anlass genug, die weltweit erste Überblicksausstellung zum Werk von Assemble zu machen. Wieso aber stelle ich diese Ausstellung an den Beginn meiner Direktion im Architekturzentrum Wien?

Seit meinem Amtsantritt wurde ich tatsächlich öfters gefragt, ob ich ein Architekturmuseum programmieren werde, das auch für Nicht-Architekt*innen interessant ist. Hat sich die Architektur soweit vom Alltag entfernt? Erwartet sich die Gesellschaft nichts mehr von der Architektur? Damit möchte ich mich nicht abfinden und stelle deshalb die Frage „Was kann Architektur?" in das Zentrum der Neuausrichtung. Das „Können" bezieht sich dabei zuallererst auf die Rückgewinnung der Handlungsfähigkeit. In den letzten Jahren hat sich unter Architekt*innen ein Gefühl der Ohnmacht breit gemacht: Zu übermächtig scheint der bauindustrielle Komplex, zu überreguliert das System, zu desinteressiert an Qualität und Baukultur wirken viele Enscheidungsträger*innen. Assemble haben sich zum Ziel gesetzt, ein starkes Stück Handlungsfähigkeit zurückzuerlangen. Mit ihrem ausdrücklichen und doch pragmatischen Optimismus arbeiten sie an der Wende von einer investorengeleiteten zu einer nutzergetriebenen Architektur und Stadtentwicklung. Dazu gehören neue Formate für Koautor*innenschaft und Koproduktion und die Bildung von neuen Allianzen über die eigene Community hinaus.

„Können" bedeutet auch, über die entsprechende Kunstfertigkeit und das Wissen zu verfügen. Was kann das Material? Was kann die

Form? Beeindruckend, zum Beispiel, wie beim Blackhorse Workshop mit wenigen Eingriffen eine Atmosphäre entstand, die das genderpolitisch Eingeübte und Gewohnte überschreitet. Und tatsächlich waren beim Lokalaugenschein auffallend viele Frauen am Werken. Und was kann Solidarität? Seit den 1960er-Jahren haben wir in mehreren Wellen den Trend zur Bildung von Kollektiven erlebt, manchmal im Gestus von Rockbands, manchmal als smarte diversifizierte Start-ups. Assemble hatten von Anfang an nicht nur ihr eigenes Kollektiv im Auge, sondern legen es darauf an, Allianzen mit anderen Gruppen zu bilden, wie zum Beispiel dem Community Land Trust in Liverpool. „Assemble sind Architekt*innen", so eine lokale Aktivistin, die „die Stimmen, Träume und Fähigkeiten der anderen hören und sehen". Es ist dieses komplexe Können, das poetisch aufgeladene, sozial vielfältige und resiliente Architektur hervorbringt.

„Was kann Architektur?" bedeutet darüber hinaus, zu fragen, was möglich, was denkbar und machbar sein könnte. Das eröffnet eine spekulative Beziehung zur Wirklichkeit. Wie würde zum Beispiel eine von Kindern mitgeplante Architektur ausschauen? Weil sich das Medium Sprache als ungeeignet für Mitsprache erwies – wie übrigens oft bei Beteiligungsprozessen – werden die 6- bis 12-Jährigen beim Baltic Street Adventure Playground dazu angeregt, sich selbst zu organisieren und mitzubauen. „Better a broken bone than a broken spirit", so das Leitmotiv des Abenteuerspielplatzes von Assemble, bei dem die Kinder beides, ihre sozialen Beziehungen und ihre gebaute Umwelt, täglich mitgestalten können. Wetterfeste Kleidung und Gummistiefel werden gestellt.

In der Ausstellung „Assemble. Wie wir bauen" im Architekturzentrum Wien werden zehn ausgewählte Projekte in großmaßstäblichen Installationen räumlich erlebbar. Videos, Zeichnungen und andere Dokumentationen machen nachvollziehbar, in welchen gemeinschaftlichen Prozessen die Materialien zusammenfinden. Materialproben fügen eine haptische Ebene hinzu. Diese Publikation in der Az W-Reihe *Hintergrund* ist als Nachhall gedacht, soll aber auch all jenen, die nicht dabei sein können, einen ersten Einblick in die Arbeit von Assemble geben. Weiters werden in der Publikation Materialien aus einer einjährigen Gastprofessur von Assemble in Wien aufgearbeitet. Bereits in den ersten Vorgesprächen zur Ausstellung war es mir ein Anliegen, nicht nur eine Dokumentation ihrer Werke, sondern auch die Arbeitsweise von Assemble nach Wien zu holen. Dieser Wunsch konnte in einer Kooperation mit der Fakultät für Architektur und Raumplanung der Technischen Universität Wien realisiert werden. Gemeinsam mit den Studierenden und David Calas als lokalem Lehrenden stellten Assemble die Frage: „Wie baut Wien?" Eine intensive architektonische Recherche zur historischen Stofflichkeit der Stadt rückte das Material Ziegel und seine sozialen, ökonomischen und ökologischen Kontexte in den Fokus. Im zweiten Semester wurden die Studierenden zum Selbstbaukollektiv: Wie könnte Wien bauen? Gemeinsam entwarfen sie einen Pavillon für den Hof des Architekturzentrum Wien, der mit den Materialien Ziegel und Lehm experimentiert und im Selbstbau errichtet wird. Mit seinem integrierten Brennofen wird er über die Sommermonate selbst wieder zu einer Werkstatt für neue Produktionsexperimente, zu denen zahlreiche Workshops einladen.

Wenn diese Publikation erscheint, sind die Bauarbeiten für den Pavillon noch in vollem Gange und dauern bewusst bis drei Wochen nach der Ausstellungseröffnung an. Der kollektive Bauprozess wird Teil der Ausstellung. Der Pavillon ist aber nicht nur öffentliche Werkstatt, sondern auch ein einladender, luftiger Ort im sommerlichen MuseumsQuartier, um gemeinsam darüber nachzudenken, was Architektur zum guten Leben beitragen kann, ob mit oder ohne Hammer in der Hand.

Aus der Frage „Was kann Architektur?" wurde also auch die Frage: „Was kann eine Architekturausstellung?" Mein Dank gilt allen Beteiligten, die sich auf dieses Abenteuer eingelassen haben. Ganz besonders möchte ich Assemble, insbesondere Maria Lisogorskaya und Lewis Jones, für die intensive und inspirierende Zusammenarbeit danken; der TU Wien, namentlich Dekan Rudolf Scheuvens und Studiendekan Christian Kühn, sowie dem future.lab und der in Kooperation mit der Stadt Wien etablierten Wissensplattform „Öffentlicher Raum", dem Institut für Kunst und Gestaltung, David Calas und allen Studierenden. Ebenfalls danken möchte ich der Wienerberger Ziegelindustrie GmbH und insbesondere Vanessa Rausch für die Unterstützung sowie der CREAU, Lukas Böckle, für die Nutzung der Werkstatträume. Ein großer Dank gilt meiner Mitkuratorin Katharina Ritter, den Autor*innen dieser Publikation, Sonja Pisarik für die Redaktion und dem gesamten Team des Architekturzentrum Wien, mit dem die Koproduktion täglich Freude macht.

Angelika Fitz,
Wien, März 2017

22 | Oliver Wainwright, Snapshots of the possible

Completed auditorium
of the Cineroleum in daylight
Der Kinosaal des Cineroleum
bei Tageslicht

Snapshots of the possible

Momentaufnahmen des Möglichen

Collaborative construction and collective action in the work of Assemble. A colourful pile of wonky ceramic tiles lies next to a gigantic stuffed giraffe in a former school changing room in south London, where desks and computers now mingle with experimental terrazzo samples strewn across the floor. In the old dance studio next door, someone is up a ladder erecting the framework for a new pottery workshop, while others manhandle a freshly cast toilet bowl into a kiln. A cauldron of spicy tofu bubbles on the stove nearby, ready for the daily team lunch.

This busy scene of making and doing is the new home of Assemble, the young archi-

Kollaboratives Bauen und gemeinschaftliches Handeln in der Arbeit von Assemble. Ein bunter Haufen Keramikfliesen liegt neben einer riesigen ausgestopften Giraffe in der Garderobe einer früheren Schule in Südlondon, wo Schreibtische und Computer sich den Raum mit experimentellen Terrazzoprobestücken teilen. Im ehemaligen Tanzstudio nebenan steht jemand auf der Leiter und baut den Rahmen für eine neue Keramikwerkstatt, während andere eine frisch gegossene Toilettenschüssel in einen Brennofen verfrachten. Auf dem nahen Herd blubbert ein Riesentopf mit würzigem Tofu und wartet auf das tägliche Mittagessen des Teams.

tecture collective that took the world by surprise last year when they scooped the Turner Prize, Europe's highest accolade for contemporary art – awarded for a project whose ambition couldn't have been any less aimed at the art-world elite.

In a run-down, mostly boarded-up corner of Liverpool's Toxteth neighbourhood, an area long trampled by failed regeneration plans, Assemble had been quietly working with the local community to devise a strategy for the incremental improvement of the area. The few remaining residents had already begun a process of guerrilla gardening to green their streets and established a monthly market, but most of the homes were empty and in dire need of repair. Making the most of what was already there, Assemble begun renovating a group of derelict terraced houses with a strategy of light-touch intervention, establishing a workshop in one of the empty homes to craft fixtures and fittings. It was part architecture, part hands-on making, part socio-economic strategy, a compelling combination that has become the hallmark of the way the group works.

Diese geschäftige Szene des Tuns und Machens ist die neue Heimat von Assemble, dem jungen Architekturkollektiv, das letztes Jahr zur großen Überraschung der Welt den Turner-Preis, Europas höchste Auszeichnung für zeitgenössische Kunst, bekam. Noch dazu erhielten Assemble den Preis für ein Projekt, das so gar nicht an die Elite der Kunstwelt adressiert war.

In einer heruntergekommenen, großteils mit Brettern verschlagenen Reihenhaussiedlung im Liverpooler Stadtteil Toxteth, einem Gebiet das unter den jahrelangen (An-)Schlägen gescheiterter Stadterneuerungspläne in die Knie gegangen war, begannen Assemble in aller Stille gemeinsam mit den Bewohner*innen eine schrittweise Revitalisierung. Zwar hatten die verbliebenen Bewohner*innen bereits eine Guerilla-Gardening-Aktion zur Begrünung der Straßen gestartet und auch einen monatlichen Markt ins Leben gerufen, aber die meisten Reihenhäuser standen leer und waren extrem reparaturbedürftig. Unter Einbeziehung der bereits geleisteten Arbeit begannen Assemble, eine Reihe der verlassenen Wohnhäuser mit sanften Eingriffen zu

Established less than seven years ago, and formalised as a company even more recently, Assemble's current projects already range from a £2m art gallery for Goldsmiths University in London, to a brewery in Japan, to a community arts centre in the US. They're now in the envious situation of having to turn down more projects (and jaunts on the international lecture circuit) than they can accept. None of the 18-strong group imagined they would be in this position when they came together in an abandoned petrol station in east London in the summer of 2010.

As a bunch of recent graduates, mostly fresh from the architecture course at University of Cambridge, but also including students of sociology, philosophy, history, and literature in their number, they joined forces out of a simple desire to build something, after years of conjuring imaginary student projects on the drawing board. Using a low-tech palette of scaffolding poles and boards, they transformed the Clerkenwell petrol station into a temporary roadside cinema, but with a level of finesse far beyond your usual "pop-up" project or student installation.

renovieren. In einem der leer stehenden Häuser errichteten sie eine Werkstatt, um dort fehlende Ausstattungsteile herzustellen. Teils Architektur, teils Selbermachprojekt, teils sozioökonomische Strategie – so lautet die faszinierende Kombination, die zum Markenzeichen dieses Kollektivs geworden ist.

Assemble gründeten ihr Kollektiv vor weniger als sieben Jahren und sind noch kürzer als eingetragenes Unternehmen tätig, und dennoch findet sich auf ihrer Auftragsliste bereits eine Kunstgalerie für die Goldsmiths University in London im Wert von zwei Millionen Pfund, eine Brauerei in Japan und ein kommunales Kunstzentrum in den USA. Sie sind jetzt schon in der beneidenswerten Lage, mehr Projekte (und Einladungen zu internationalen Vorträgen) ablehnen zu müssen, als sie annehmen können. Keines der Mitglieder dieses 18-köpfigen Kollektivs hätte sich diese Situation träumen lassen, als sie im Sommer 2010 in einer verlassenen Tankstelle im Osten Londons ihre Arbeit aufnahmen.

Die Gruppe von Universitätsabsolvent*innen, die meisten von der Architekturfakultät in Cambridge, aber auch Absolvent*innen

Sheets of Tyvek, the foil-like waterproof building material, were turned into walls of sumptuous silvery swagged curtains, hoisted in a dramatic reveal at the end of each screening to leave the audience exposed on the edge of a busy main road. Formica was used to make intricate marquetry tops for tables and stools, while decorative plastic tiles were vacuum-formed on site, using a jury-rigged hot air gun and a vacuum cleaner, to transform the ceiling of the former garage shop into something special. It showed what was possible with a bit of imagination and collective action, providing a snapshot of an alternative future for this left-over slice of the street.

It was a simple, short-lived thing, but the Cineroleum embodied the kind of attention to detail, craft, wit and the collective theatre of making as a performance in itself, that has gone on to define everything Assemble does. The building site became a live laboratory of experimentation and testing, a festival of learning by trial and error and forum for meeting others who wanted to get involved.

Following the success of this fleeting filmic apparition, the group (as yet unnamed)

der Soziologie, Philosophie, Geschichte und Literatur, tat sich zusammen, weil sie nach Jahren der imaginären Student*innenprojekte endlich wirklich etwas bauen wollten. Mit Low-Tech-Materialien wie Gerüststangen und -brettern verwandelten sie die Tankstelle in der Clerkenwell Road in ein temporäres Kino, bewiesen dabei allerdings ein Maß an Raffinesse, das weit über die üblichen „Pop-up"-Projekte oder Student*inneninstallationen hinausging.

Aus langen Tyvekbahnen, einer folienartigen wasserdichten Dachmembran, wurden üppig gebauschte, silbrige Vorhangwände, die nach dem Ende der Filmvorführung in dramatischer Inszenierung hochgezogen wurden, um das Publikum wieder ins Hier und Jetzt einer belebten Straßenszenerie zu entlassen. Aus Formica-Laminat entstanden feine Intarsienarbeiten für Tischplatten, während dekorative Plastikfliesen mit einer Kombination aus Heißluftpistole und Staubsauger an Ort und Stelle vakuumverformt wurden, um der Decke des früheren Tankstellenshops neuen Glanz zu verleihen. Dieses Projekt zeigte, was mithilfe von etwas Fantasie und kollektiver Mithilfe möglich ist

applied for funding from east London arts charity Create to build another temporary performance and screening space, this time beneath a motorway flyover in an unlikely corner of the Lea Valley, near where the site of the 2012 Olympic Games was being summoned from the mud. Conceived as a little house trapped beneath the roads, the Folly for a Flyover poked its pitched roof up between the roaring lanes of traffic like a fairy-tale cottage gone astray. Made of wooden bricks sawn from railway sleepers and hung like drapery over a scaffolding frame, it was built by an army of 200 volunteers and provided a surreal theatrical setting for films,

und bot eine Vorschau auf eine potenzielle alternative Zukunft für dieses ungenutzte Straßengrundstück.

Das Cineroleum war ein einfaches, temporäres Projekt, wies aber schon alle Aspekte auf, die die Arbeitsweise von Assemble prägen: Liebe zum Detail, handwerkliches Geschick, Humor und die performative Inszenierung des gemeinschaftlichen Selbermachens. Die Baustelle wurde zum lebendigen Testlabor, zu einem Fest des Lernens durch Versuch und Irrtum, und zu einem Forum, um Gleichgesinnte kennenzulernen.

Nach dem Erfolg dieser flüchtigen Kinoerscheinung suchte die (noch namenlose)

Folly for a flyover at night
during a performance
Folly unter einer Autobahnbrücke
während einer nächtlichen Vorführung

talks and children's play sessions over the summer. While the Olympic steamroller was busy flattening this curious edge-land of workshops and warehouses beneath its sterile carpet, the Folly had a remarkable handmade delicacy, standing as a carefully crafted foil to the brute concrete infrastructure through which it was woven. A raised stage of colourful terrazzo tiles still stands on the site today, as a playful reminder of what once happened here, and a prompt for what might come next. One recent spring weekend, a couple were using it as an impromptu outdoor workshop for fixing their boat, moored next to the stage on the River Lea.

In both these initial temporary projects and the more permanent work that has come since, there is an evident joy in the process of construction. The meticulous material enquiries are as much a driver as the bigger social ideas that the projects explore. The members' lack of conventional training as carpenters, ceramicists, or bricklayers means that they approach their building materials with an inquisitive, sideways view, and the results are often disarmingly poetic. Why use off-the-peg tiles, when you can cast

Gruppe bei der Ostlondoner Kunst-Charity Create um Geldmittel für einen weiteren Performanceraum an: diesmal unter einer Autobahnbrücke in einem unattraktiven Eck von Lea Valley, in der Nähe des Geländes, auf dem die Sportstätten für die Olympiade 2012 aus dem schlammigen Boden gestampft wurden. Konzipiert als kleines Gebäude unter der Autobahn, mutete Folly for a Flyover mit seinem vorwitzig zwischen den vorbeisausenden Autos hervorgestreckten Spitzdach wie ein verirrtes Knusperhäuschen an. Die Wände bestanden aus einer vorhangartigen Konstruktion mit Holzziegeln aus zersägten Eisenbahnschwellen, die über einem Baugerüstrahmen aufgespannt wurde. Von einer Armee von 200 Freiwilligen errichtet, diente Folly einen Sommer lang als surreale Bühne für Filmvorführungen, Vorträge und Kinderspiele. Im Unterschied zur olympischen Dampfwalze, die gnadenlos über dieses Randgebiet mit seinen Werkstätten und Lagerhäusern hinwegrollte, war Folly von außergewöhnlicher handgemachter Zartheit und bot einen inszenierten Kontrast zur brutalen Betoninfrastruktur, in die es eingefügt worden

your own and enjoy the irregular, haphazard finish? Why use a prefabricated perforated screen when you can blast corrugated sheeting with a shotgun to create a beguiling constellation of tiny randomised holes? Working with an almost alchemical sensibility from first principles, they have developed strange hybrid materials, like "paper-crete" for a series of exhibition tables, and rugged "rubble-dash" render to bring an archaic, primal air to a little temple-like music venue for Cafe Oto in Dalston.

These curious outcomes are often the result of collaboration with other artists, makers and builders. Their open-minded, no-holds-barred approach fosters an inquisitive, can-do attitude to the way in which things might be assembled and processes developed. Indeed their name, Assemble – which was finally settled on after lengthy discussions worthy of the Vatican council – reflects how their work is about bringing things together in different, unexpected ways, be they people, materials or ideas. Not everything is drawn from the beginning, but evolves on site, in an iterative, incremental way, informed by continuous prototyping back in the studio.

war. Die Bühnenkonstruktion aus bunten Terrazzofliesen ist als Erinnerung und als Vorzeichen für mögliche Zukunftsentwicklungen stehen geblieben. Vor Kurzem verwendete ein Pärchen den Ort an einem Frühlingswochenende als improvisierte Werkstatt, um ihr Boot instand zu setzen, das gleich daneben am Ufer des Flüsschens Lea festgemacht war.

Diesen temporären, wie auch den folgenden dauerhaften Projekten sieht man die Freude am Konstruktionsprozess deutlich an. Die ausgeklügelten Materialexperimente sind genauso Motivation wie die dahinterstehenden sozialen Anliegen. Da die Mitglieder des Kollektivs keine Ausbildung als Tischler, Keramiker oder Maurer genossen haben, gehen sie mit neugieriger Unvoreingenommenheit an ihre Baustoffe heran und erzielen damit oft erstaunlich poetische Ergebnisse. Warum Fliesen kaufen, wenn man sie selbst herstellen und sich an der unregelmäßigen Zufälligkeit des Ergebnisses erfreuen kann? Warum fertiges Lochblech verwenden, wenn man mit einer Schrotflinte reizvolle Zufallskonstellationen von winzigen Löchern in ein Wellblech schießen kann?

Europa's graphic design
for the Blackhorse Workshop
Europas Grafikdesign für den
Blackhorse Workshop

Mit geradezu alchemistischer Begeisterung überdenkt das Kollektiv auch noch die grundlegendsten Prinzipien und hat auf diese Weise die wundersamsten Hybridmaterialien hervorgebracht, wie zum Beispiel *paper-crete* („Papierbeton") für eine Serie von Ausstellungstischen, oder *rubble-dash* (Rauputz aus Bauschutt), mit dem sie einer kleinen Spielstätte für das Cafe OTO in Dalston einen archaischen Anstrich verliehen.

Diese unorthodoxen Eigenfabrikate entstehen oft in Zusammenarbeit mit anderen Künstler*innen, Handwerker*innen und Baufachleuten. Die unvoreingenommene und beherzte Can-do-Haltung des Kollektivs prägt auch die Entwicklung ihrer Konstruktionsmethoden. Schon der Name Assemble – auf den sie sich erst nach Diskussionen von der Langwierigkeit eines vatikanischen Konzils einigten – zeigt, dass es ihnen darum geht, Menschen, Materialien und Ideen in neuen, überraschenden Konstellationen zusammenzufügen. Bei Weitem nicht alles entsteht schon am Reißbrett, vieles entwickelt sich vor Ort in einem schrittweisen Prozess, der auch vom laufenden Prototyping im Atelier profitiert.

It is spaciousness of their studio, with ready access to tools for woodworking, metalworking, casting and firing, which has proved to be crucial in fostering this hands-on, tactile way of working. After scouring London to find a space, the group's watershed moment came in 2012 with the arrival of the Olympics. The accompanying circus of regeneration came with small pots of funding to seed community arts projects in the area surrounding the Olympic Park, which was intentionally sited at the nexus of three of London's poorest boroughs. As part of the programme in the "Olympic fringe", Assemble were lucky enough to land a free warehouse, along with funding to do it up as their studio and events space. Sited on Stratford's Sugarhouse Lane, an area of old industrial sheds and workshops that was soon to be developed into a mixed-use vision by Ikea's property development arm, this gritty location gave them the space and freedom to experiment at a bigger scale. With ping-pong tables, a cafe and small auditorium, it evolved into a lively hub of activity, allowing them to subsidise their work by opening a bar and throwing wild parties (even if

Es ist die Geräumigkeit ihres Ateliers, mit Zugang zu Werkzeugen für Holz- und Metallbearbeitung, Gießen und Brennen, die sich als essenziell für die taktile, praxisnahe Arbeitsweise erwiesen hat. Nachdem sie lange auf der Suche nach geeigneten Räumlichkeiten in London waren, stellten die Olympischen Spiele 2012 den Wendepunkt dar. Der damit einhergehende Stadterneuerungszirkus brachte Fördertöpfe für lokale Kunstprojekte rund um das Olympia-Gelände, das bewusst am Kreuzungspunkt der drei ärmsten Bezirke von London angesiedelt war. Assemble hatten das Glück, ein leer stehendes Lagerhaus sowie die für die Adaptierung nötigen Fördermittel zu ergattern. Das Gelände an der Sugarhouse Lane in Stratford mit seinen alten Werkstätten stand kurz davor, von Ikeas Immobilienzweig erschlossen zu werden. Diese nicht gerade luxuriöse Location eröffnete Assemble den Raum und die Freiheit für Experimente in größerem Maßstab. Tischtennistische, ein Café und ein Vortragssaal waren die Ausstattung für ihren lebendigen Aktionsraum, und mit der Eröffnung einer Bar und der Veranstaltung von wilden Partys besserten

making sourdough pizzas wasn't quite as easy or lucrative as they had hoped).

Having proved themselves, they applied for further funding from the Olympic legacy corporation to build another shed in their yard to house affordable studio space for other local artists and makers. But it wasn't to be any old shed. Erected with the collective spirit of an Amish barn-raising, the Yardhouse took the form of a timber-framed hangar, its two floors of studios arranged around a processional staircase, with elegantly welded chandelier light-fittings, and clad with a facade of handmade candy-coloured cement tiles. The startling pastel backdrop soon became an accidental Instagram sensation, turning this East End industrial estate into an unlikely place of pilgrimage for the selfie brigade.

Their lease here came to an end last year, but the four-year experiment of Sugarhouse Studios made Assemble realise that what they had created was bigger than the practice itself, having spawned an energetic community of like-minded makers. Seeing the need for similar spaces elsewhere, they developed a plan for another more public

sie ihre Finanzen auf (auch wenn die Herstellung von Sauerteigpizzas sich als nicht ganz so einfach oder lukrativ erwies, wie sie gehofft hatten).

Nach dieser Bewährung beantragten sie Fördermittel von der Olympic Legacy Corporation, um in ihrem Hinterhof leistbare Arbeitsräume für ortsansässige Künstler*innen und Handwerker*innen zu errichten. Im typischen Gemeinschaftsgeist entstand so Yardhouse: eine Holzrahmenkonstruktion in Form eines Hangars mit Atelierräumen auf zwei Geschossen und einem zentralen Gemeinschaftsraum mit elegantem Treppenaufstieg und kronleuchterartigen Beleuchtungskörpern. Die Außenfassade ist mit handgemachten Zementfliesen in Bonbonfarben verkleidet. Dieser unvermutet pastellbunte Anblick avancierte sofort zu einer Sensation auf Instagram und machte das Industriegelände im Londoner East End zur Pilgerstätte für die Selfie-Brigade.

Ihr Mietvertrag lief letztes Jahr aus, aber im Zuge dieses vierjährigen Experiments erkannten Assemble, dass ihre Arbeiten eine Strahlkraft entwickelten, die über den eigentlichen Rahmen der Projekte hinausging

workshop building further north, in Walthamstow, securing money from the mayor's Outer London Fund to realise Blackhorse Workshop, which has since become a thriving centre of designers, carpenters, and metalworkers, counting 800 members three years on.

The process of seeding such projects has required a level of on-going commitment far beyond the usual architect's role, and beyond what Assemble ever anticipated. They initiated a similar bottom-up community project in Glasgow, also funded by Create, to establish a children's adventure playground in Dalmarnock, one of the most deprived parts of the city where average life expectancy is below 60 years. It seemed that the vast stadia of the 2014 Commonwealth Games were not going to do much to help: instead the masterplan bulldozed the local shop and cafe, and crushed fine Victorian tenement buildings beneath an inward-looking campus of gleaming new sports venues.

Granby Four Streets,
Liverpool

und eine Community von gleichgesinnten „Makers" ins Leben gerufen hatte. Da sie erkannten, dass auch anderswo ähnliche Aktionsräume gebraucht werden, sicherten sie sich Geldmittel aus dem Outer London Fund des Bürgermeisters und realisierten Blackhorse Workshop, eine offene Werkstatt weiter nördlich in Walthamstow, die sich in den letzten drei Jahren zu einem florierenden Zentrum für Designer*innen, Tischler*innen und Schlosser*innen mit nunmehr 800 Mitgliedern entwickelt hat.

Projekte dieser Art zu entwickeln, erforderte ein Maß an Engagement, das weit über die übliche Rolle des Architekten hinausging und auch weit mehr war, als Assemble sich je vorgestellt hatten. Ein ähnliches Bottom-up-Gemeinschaftsprojekt realisierten sie in Glasgow. Hier entstand, mit Fördermitteln von Create, ein Abenteuerspielplatz in Dalmarnock, einem der benachteiligsten Stadtteile mit einer durchschnittlichen Lebenserwartung von weniger als 60 Jahren. Die riesigen Stadien, die dort im Zuge der Commonwealth Games 2014 emporwuchsen, erwiesen sich als wenig hilfreich für die Aufwertung der Nachbarschaft: Gemäß

34 | Oliver Wainwright, Snapshots of the possible

Street view of terraced
housing stock in Granby
Straßenansicht eines bestehenden
Reihenhauses in Granby

In an alternative model of urban acupuncture on a small piece of land across the street from the stadia, Assemble showed how, with a shoestring budget and a lot of "sweat equity", a small-scale intervention could have a lasting impact for the neighbourhood. Eschewing the usual play equipment for a more DIY approach, Baltic Street playground has been about encouraging kids to get their hands dirty and build structures for themselves, making dens and tyre swings and cooking around a camp fire, an essential provision in an area where some children don't get a hot meal every day. One of the most important outcomes has been about capacity-building in the local community: over the last three years, Assemble have helped to source funding and train a pair of play-workers, who now have the skills to run the project for themselves. Rather than coming up with a grand design and having it implemented, they laid the foundations that enabled the local residents do it for themselves, empowering the children and demonstrating how it's possible for them to shape their physical environment from an early age.

Masterplan wurde der örtliche Nahversorger samt Café abgerissen und schöne viktorianische Wohnhäuser unter einem abgeschotteten Campus mit chromglänzenden Sportstätten begraben.

Mit einem Alternativmodell für urbane Akupunktur auf dem kleinen Gelände auf der den Stadien gegenüberliegenden Straßenseite demonstrierten Assemble, wie man mit einem Minibudget und viel „Schweiß- und Muskelkapital" eine kleinräumige, aber nachhaltige Intervention auf die Beine stellt. Sie verzichteten auf die übliche Spielplatzausstattung zugunsten eines Do-it-yourself-Ansatzes. Beim Spielplatz in der Baltic Street werden Kinder ermutigt, sich die Hände schmutzig zu machen und ihre eigenen Strukturen zu errichten, Höhlen und Reifenschaukeln zu bauen und am Lagerfeuer Essen zuzubereiten. Letzteres stellt in einem Gebiet, in dem manche Kinder nicht jeden Tag warmes Essen bekommen, ein essenzielles Angebot dar. Eines der wichtigsten Ergebnisse war der Aufbau von Kapazitäten in der örtlichen Gemeinschaft: In den letzten drei Jahren haben Assemble mitgeholfen, zwei Spielplatzbetreuer*innen zu finanzieren und auszubilden,

Working model 1:10 of a terraced house on Cairns Street
Arbeitsmodell 1:10 eines Hauses in der Cairns Street

die nun das Projekt selbstständig betreiben können. Anstatt mit einem großspurigen Plan aufzuwarten und diesen umsetzen zu lassen, legten sie den Grundstein, der die örtliche Bevölkerung befähigte, selbst tätig zu werden und den Kindern zeigte, wie sie schon in jungen Jahren ihre physische Umgebung gestalten können.

Dieser partizipatorische Anspruch ist ein Grundelement in allen Arbeiten von Assemble. Sie wollen den Menschen wieder nahebringen, wie gestaltbar Lebensräume sind. Mit kollaborativen Aktionen demonstrieren ihre Projekte, dass eine Stadt nicht ganz so festgeschrieben ist, wie man glauben möchte, sondern vielmehr ein Raum im Fluss ist, eine Reihe von Gelegenheiten, die nur darauf warten, ergriffen zu werden. Einer langen britischen Tradition von William Morris bis Walter Segal folgend, setzen sie den Prozess des Selbermachens und des gemeinschaftlichen Bauens ein, um alternative soziale und politische Ambitionen zu verwirklichen. Ihre Projekte sind Prototypen von möglichen Zukünften, ein optimistischer Anstoß, sich alternative Wege für das Bauen einer Gesellschaft vorzustellen.

It is a participatory ambition that underlies all of their work, aiming to address the usual disconnection between people and the way in which their neighbourhoods are made. Through collaborative action, their projects demonstrate that the city isn't quite as fixed as you might think, but instead a place of flux and change, a series of opportunities waiting to happen. Following a rich English tradition, from William Morris to Walter Segal, they use the process of making and direct collective construction to express alternative social and political aspirations. Their projects are prototypes of possible futures, optimistic provocations to imagine different ways that society could build.

In a stratospheric trajectory that would take most practices a decade or two to achieve, Assemble have gone from a temporary installation in a petrol station to winning multi-million-pound arts commissions and being chased by high-profile clients the world over. Given all the attention, is their model of agile project-initiating, community skills-building and collective making a sustainable form of practice? And how will it

In einem stratosphärischen Werdegang, für den andere Architekturbüros ein bis zwei Jahrzehnte brauchen würden, sind Assemble von einer temporären Installation in einer Tankstelle zu hochbegehrten Gestalter*innen avanciert, die millionenschwere Aufträge erhalten und von international hochrangigen Auftraggeber*innen angefragt werden. Angesichts des Aufsehens, das sie erregen, stellt sich die Frage, ob ihr Modell des agilen Initiierens von Projekten mit lokalem Skill-Building und kollektivem Selbermachen eine nachhaltige Praxis darstellt? Wie wird es weitergehen, wenn die Gruppe weiter wächst und sich weit größerer Projekte annimmt?

Im Moment ernährt das Unternehmen seine 15 Vollzeitdirektor*innen, wobei die meisten von ihnen auch unterrichten, sowie einige teilzeitbeschäftigte und freiberufliche Mitarbeiter*innen. Sie räumen allerdings ein, dass sie Schwierigkeiten haben, ein vernünftiges Einkommen zu erzielen und die Zeit zu finden, sich wirklich mit den unzähligen spannenden Projekten auseinanderzusetzen, die man ihnen anbietet.

Seit ihren Anfängen hat die Gruppe zwar gewisse Strukturen eingeführt (vor einein-

evolve as the group matures and takes on larger-scale projects?

For now, the practice can sustain its 15 full-time directors, most of whom also teach for a day a week, along with several other part-time and freelance workers. They do, however, admit that they are struggling to find a way to make enough money to pay themselves properly, or to find the time to take on the innumerable exciting projects that keep coming their way.

The group has certainly formalised its way of working since their early beginnings (they hired an office manager a year and a half ago), but their outlook has barely changed since they sat in a circle beneath the petrol station roof and made every decision by collective consensus. Projects are now run by pairs of project leaders, but everyone stays involved in what's going on through the weekly Monday meetings and regular design charrettes. They have also realised that their strength for research, analysis, and brief development could be a valuable branch of the business in itself, and they are busy setting up their own construction company too. It is a sensible move, given that our

halb Jahren stellten sie einen Büroleiter ein), aber ihr Ansatz hat sich kaum geändert seit der Zeit, als sie im Kreis unter dem Tankstellendach saßen und jede Entscheidung im Kollektiv getroffen wurde. Projekte werden nun von zwei Projektleiter*innen betreut, aber immer noch sind alle daran beteiligt, ob bei den wöchentlichen Montagsmeetings oder den regelmäßigen Design-Charrettes. Sie haben auch erkannt, dass ihr Talent für Recherchen, Analyse und kurze Entwicklung einen wertvollen eigenständigen Geschäftszweig darstellen könnte und sind dabei, ihr eigenes Bauunternehmen zu gründen. Ein vernünftiger Schritt angesichts unserer risikofeindlichen Beschaffungskultur, in der so viele Projekte von den Generalunternehmen bestimmt werden und Architekt*innen nur mehr den Bauunternehmen zuarbeiten.

Und hat der Turner-Preis sie verändert? Es genügt vielleicht, zu wissen, dass sie keine Ahnung hatten, wer die Anruferin war, als die Direktorin von Tate Britain sich mit der guten Nachricht bei ihnen meldete. Sie verdrehen die Augen, wenn man das „T-Wort" erwähnt: Offensichtlich sind sie es leid, dar-

risk-averse procurement culture means that so many projects are now contractor-led, with the architect subservient to the builder.

And has the Turner Prize changed them? Perhaps it tells you all you need to know that when the director of Tate Britain called to give them the news, they didn't know who she was. They roll their eyes when you mention the T-word; they're clearly sick of talking about it. After all, they've got far too much real work to be getting on with. There's a world out there to fix.

Oliver Wainwright is the architecture and design critic of the Guardian. He trained as an architect, he has worked for a number of practices, including OMA, muf and Design for London. He has written extensively on architecture and urbanism for a wide range of international publications and is a regular visiting critic and lecturer at several architecture schools.

über zu reden. Schließlich haben sie viel zu viel wirkliche Arbeit zu erledigen. Da draußen ist eine Welt, die es zu reparieren gilt.

Oliver Wainwright ist Architektur- und Designkritiker des Guardian. Nach der Architekturausbildung war er für einige Architekturbüros tätig, darunter OMA, muf architecture / art und Design for London. Er ist der Verfasser zahlreicher Beiträge über Architektur und Urbanismus für eine Vielzahl von internationalen Publikationen und ist regelmäßiger Gastkritiker und Gastdozent an mehreren Architekturfakultäten.

---

40 | The Cineroleum

Abandoned petrol station
on Clerkenwell Road, London
Aufgelassene Tankstelle
an der Clerkenwell Road, London

The Cineroleum

The Cineroleum was a temporary, self-initiated project that transformed a derelict petrol station on Clerkenwell Road into a cinema. The project was an experiment in the potential for the wider re-use of the UK's 4,000 empty petrol stations.

The Cineroleum was an improvisation on the rich iconography and decadent interiors of the golden age picture palace. Classic elements were re-created for the roadside setting using cheap industrial, reclaimed, or

Das Cineroleum verwandelte eine aufgelassene Tankstelle an der Clerkenwell Road in ein Kino. Mit diesem temporären und eigeninitiierten Projekt wollten Assemble aufzeigen, welch großes Potenzial für neue Nutzungen in den 4.000 brachliegenden Tankstellen Großbritanniens steckt.

Den Gestalter*innen bot sich hier die Gelegenheit zur Auseinandersetzung mit der üppigen Ikonografie und den dekadenten Interieurs der Filmpaläste aus der Glanzzeit des Kinos. Klassische Ausstattungselemente wurden passend zum Standort mit billigen Industrie- und Recyclingwerkstoffen und geschenkten Materialien nachempfunden.

Site / Ort:
100 Clerkenwell Road, London
Year / Jahr:
2010
Client / Auftraggeber:
Self-initiated

At the end of the film the curtain was lifted, pushing the audience from the imaginative world of the film to the everyday theatre of the street.

donated materials. Flip-up seats were made from scaffolding boards, the foyer was furnished with formica-clad school chairs and tables, and the auditorium was enclosed by a curtain, created by hand-sewing about three kilometres of Tyvek roofing membrane.

The Cineroleum was visibly handmade, built on site by a team of over a hundred volunteers, learning and experimenting together, aided by instruction manuals written during the prototyping process.

Unlike the out-of-town multiplex, The Cineroleum celebrated the social experience of film-going, from the popcorn machine and bar in the old station shop through to

Die Klappsitze wurden aus Gerüstbrettern gefertigt, das Foyer mit Schulmöbeln aus Laminat ausgestattet, und den Zuschauerraum umschloss ein Vorhang aus etwa 3.000 Metern handvernähter Tyvek-Dachmembran.

Das Cineroleum war sichtbar handgefertigt. Ein Team, bestehend aus mehr als hundert Freiwilligen, errichtete das Kino in einem gemeinsamen Lern- und Experimentierprozess. Sie stützten sich dabei lediglich auf Montagehandbücher, die während des Prototypings erstellt wurden.

Im Unterschied zu den Multiplexkinos am Stadtrand zelebrierte das Cineroleum das soziale Erlebnis eines Kinobesuchs, von

Sewing the festoon curtain
Das Nähen des gerafften Vorhangs

the programme of approachable classics. Separated from the busiest single-lane road in Europe by a curtain, it allowed for collective escapism and created a public spectacle on the street for passers-by. At the end of the film, the curtain was lifted, pushing the audience from the imaginative world of the film to the everyday theatre of the street.

der Popcornmaschine und Bar im früheren Tankstellenshop bis zur Programmgestaltung mit beliebten Kinoklassikern. Nur durch einen Vorhang von der meistbefahrenen einspurigen Straße Europas getrennt, bot es eine Möglichkeit zum kollektiven Eskapismus und lieferte auch den Passant*innen draußen ein Spektakel. Am Ende des Films hob sich der Vorhang, und das Publikum wurde aus der imaginären Welt des Kinos ins alltägliche Schauspiel der Straße zurückgeholt.

44 | **The Cineroleum**

100 Clerkenwell Road, London | 45

The Cineroleum during a screening
Das Cineroleum während einer Filmvorführung

Entrance to the Sugarhouse Yard
Eingang zum Sugarhouse-Gelände

Sugarhouse Studios

Sugarhouse Studios is an affordable workspace complex, home to Assemble and many other designers, carpenters, and artists. The project was set up by Assemble in 2012 and takes its name from the first building it occupied – an empty light industrial unit in Sugarhouse Yard, Stratford. The space was offered to Assemble by the London Legacy Development Corporation while it awaited development by Ikea's property branch. It has since moved to occupy part of a school

Site / Ort:
Various
Year / Jahr:
2012–Ongoing
Client / Auftraggeber:
Self-initiated

Sugarhouse Studios ist ein kostengünstiger Komplex von Arbeitsräumen, der Assemble und viele andere Designer*innen, Tischler*innen und Künstler*innen beherbergt. Das 2012 von Assemble initiierte Projekt bezieht seinen Namen von dem ursprünglichen Gebäude, das es besetzte: einem verlassenen Industriegebäude am Sugarhouse Yard im Londoner Stadtteil Stratford. Das Gelände wartete damals auf Erschließung durch den Immobilienzweig von Ikea und wurde Assemble zwischenzeitlich von der London Legacy Development Corporation zur Verfügung gestellt. Inzwischen sind die Sugarhouse Studios auf einen Schulcampus

The project seeks to provide a collaborative work environment, promoting dialogue across disciplines and hosting public events alongside day-to-day working practice.

awaiting redevelopment in Bermondsey, South London and will move again in 2020 when the current site is redeveloped.

Sugarhouse provides workspace for artists, designers, musicians, and fabricators around a pool of common facilities that enable and support collaboration. These facilities, normally out of reach for individuals and small businesses include metal, wood, and ceramics workshops, meeting rooms and large-scale indoor and outdoor assembly spaces.

Sugarhouse has enabled the development of Assemble's hands-on model of practice, and it has been a base for the development

in Bermondsey in Südlondon übersiedelt. Sie werden im Jahr 2020 erneut umziehen, da der gegenwärtige Standort dann generalsaniert wird.

Sugarhouse bietet Arbeitsräume für Künstler*innen, Designer*innen, Musiker*innen und Handwerker*innen in einem kollaborativen Umfeld mit einer Reihe von gemeinschaftlich genutzten Einrichtungen, wie z. B. Holz- und Keramikwerkstätten, Besprechungsräume und groß dimensionierte Flächen für Konstruktionsarbeiten im Innenbereich und im Freien, die normalerweise für Einzelpersonen und Kleinstbetriebe unerschwinglich sind.

Material tests at the studio of Assemble
Materialexperimente im Studio von Assemble

and construction of numerous projects across the UK by Assemble and its other tenants.

The project seeks to provide a collaborative work environment, promoting dialogue across disciplines and hosting public events alongside day-to-day working practice. Since starting in 2012, the studios have supported a wide variety of uses, from kids workshops, conferences, exhibitions, educational courses to music performances, film screenings and late night events.

Sugarhouse ermöglichte die Ausarbeitung des praxisnahen Arbeitsmodells von Assemble und war Grundlage für die Entwicklung und den Bau zahlreicher Projekte in Großbritannien.

Das Projekt soll eine kollaborative Arbeitsumgebung schaffen, den Dialog über Fachbereichsgrenzen fördern und neben der täglichen Arbeitspraxis auch Raum für öffentliche Veranstaltungen bieten. Seit 2012 haben die Sugarhouse Studios eine Vielzahl von Nutzungen erlebt, von Workshops für Kinder und Konferenzen über Ausstellungen und Kurse bis zu Musikveranstaltungen, Filmvorführungen und Abendveranstaltungen.

50 | **Sugarhouse Studios**

Sugarhouse Yard, Stratford, London | 51

Sugarhouse Studios as collective
working and event spaces
Sugarhouse Studios als gemeinschaftliche
Arbeits- und Veranstaltungsräume

Yardhouse

The candy-coloured facade of cement
tiles turned into a pilgrimage for the selfie brigade.
Die bunte Fassade aus Zementfliesen
wurde zur Pilgerstätte für die Selfie-Brigade.

Yardhouse

Yardhouse is an adaptable building system developed for affordable workspace. The prototype – constructed for only £ 291/m² – was built in Sugarhouse Yard in Stratford, on one of many large-scale development sites adjacent to the Olympic Park. It is designed as a modular system that can utilise vacant plots awaiting development, before being dismantled and re-erected elsewhere.

Site / Ort:
Sugarhouse Yard,
Stratford High Street, London
Year / Jahr:
2014
Client / Auftraggeber:
Self-initiated, match-funded by London Legacy Development Corporation

Yardhouse ist ein adaptierbares Bausystem zur Schaffung von kostengünstigem Arbeitsraum. Der Prototyp entstand am Sugarhouse Yard in Stratford, einem von vielen Entwicklungsstandorten neben dem Londoner Olympiapark. Das modulare System kann auf temporär ungenutzten Flächen errichtet und, sobald diese anderweitig erschlossen werden, wieder ab- und an einem anderen Standort neu aufgebaut werden.

Die Anlage des Gebäudes fördert soziale Interaktion und Zusammenarbeit. Die schlichte scheunenartige zweigeschossige Holzrahmenkonstruktion ist mit wärmegedämmten Fertigelementen verkleidet und

Self-building construction of the studio
Der Ausbau der Ateliers erfolgt im Selbstbau.

The building provided a sociable and collaborative work environment. It was simply arranged, as a barn-like two-storey, three-bay timber structure and enclosed by prefabricated insulated panels. The two outer bays

in drei Bereiche gegliedert. Die zwei Außenflügel werden als individuelle Ateliers genutzt und öffnen sich zu einem über beide Geschosse reichenden Mittelteil, der als großzügiger Gemeinschaftsraum gestaltet ist. Die einzelnen Ateliereinheiten sind nicht durch Trennwände abgegrenzt, es steht den Mieter*innen aber frei, den Raum ihren spezifischen Anforderungen anzupassen, benachbarte Einheiten zu verbinden oder durch Abtrennungen mehr Privatsphäre zu schaffen.

Die Verwendung handelsüblicher Werkstoffe und eine extrem sparsame Konstruktionsweise ermöglichen die für kreative

Yardhouse is designed as a modular system for affordable workspace that can utilise vacant plots awaiting development, before being dismantled and re-erected elsewhere.

were used as individual studio spaces, and open onto a generous double-height communal area. Studios were provided without partitions, but tenants were free to adapt their space to suit their practice, combining adjacent units or enclosing their space for greater privacy.

Through utilising off-the-shelf materials and taking an extremely economical approach to construction, the project provided the generous scale, light quality, and ceiling heights desirable for creative uses at a fraction of the cost of a conventional new build. For the prototype located in Sugarhouse Yard, the front facade was clad in

Nutzungen erwünschte großzügige Dimension, Lichtqualität und Raumhöhe zu einem Bruchteil der Kosten eines konventionellen Neubaus. Die Frontfassade des Prototyps am Sugarhouse Yard wurde mit vor Ort handgefertigten vielfarbigen Zementfliesen gedeckt und bietet einen angemessenen Hintergrund für das öffentliche Areal, an dem das Gebäude liegt.

Für Design und Bau von Yardhouse, einschließlich Innenausbau und -ausstattung, zeichnen Assemble verantwortlich, die Innenwände wurden von den Mieter*innen errichtet. Bereits vor der Fertigstellung waren alle Flächen vollständig vermietet,

Central foyer and staircase
Zentraler Gemeinschaftsraum und Treppenaufgang

colourful concrete tiles handmade on site, forming a backdrop for the adjacent public yard.

Yardhouse was initiated, designed, and built by Assemble, including fixtures and fittings. Internal partitions are tenants' own. The building was fully let prior to completion, oversubscribed by 10 applicants for every space. The project received funding from the London Legacy Development Corporation as part of Emerging East. The prototype Yardhouse has been dismantled and moved from its original location and will be re-erected on another site in September 2017.

wobei es zehn Anwärter*innen für jeden Atelierraum gab. Die Finanzierung erfolgte mit Unterstützung von London Legacy Development Corporation im Rahmen des Stadterneuerungsprogramms Emerging East. Der Prototyp von Yardhouse wurde am ursprünglichen Standort abgebaut, die Wiedererrichtung erfolgt im September 2017 an anderer Stelle.

Celebrations in the yard
Ein Fest im Hof

58 | Yardhouse

Sugarhouse Yard, Stratford High Street, London | 59

Newly occupied workspace at Yardhouse
Bezogenes Atelier im Yardhouse

Each tile had to be screwed into timber battens.
Jede Fliese musste mit den Holzplatten
verschraubt werden.

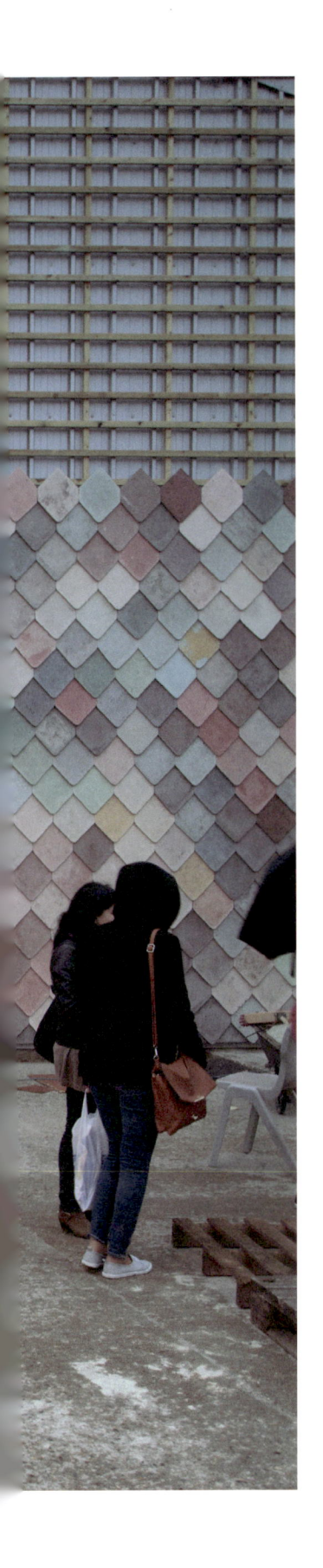

Timber workshop space at
Blackhorse Workshop
Holzwerkstatt im
Blackhorse Workshop

Blackhorse Workshop

Blackhorse Workshop is a public building in Walthamstow, which provides affordable access to tools, workspace, and on-site technical expertise. The workshop is a new type of institution, aimed at cultivating and disseminating a culture of making and mending, celebrating the area's rich history of craft and manufacturing, once the home of William Morris.

Site / Ort:
Walthamstow, London
Year / Jahr:
2014
Client / Auftraggeber:
London Borough of Waltham Forest, Greater London Authority

Blackhorse Workshop ist eine offene Werkstatt in Walthamstow, die kostengünstigen Zugang zu Werkstätten, Maschinen und Arbeitsräumen sowie Betreuung durch Fachleute anbietet. Dieser neue Typ von Einrichtung hat es sich zum Ziel gesetzt, die Kultur des Selbermachens und Reparierens zu fördern. Gleichzeitig wird damit auch die reiche Handwerks- und Manufakturtradition dieses Londoner Bezirks gewürdigt, in dem einst William Morris lebte.

Blackhorse Workshop bietet für Selbstständige und Hobbybastler*innen, Einzelunternehmer*innen und Kleinstbetriebe Raum zum Arbeiten und Lernen. Das Angebot

Blackhorse Workshop

The workshop is a new type of institution, aimed at cultivating and disseminating a culture of making and mending, celebrating the area's rich history of craft and manufacturing.

Yard of Blackhorse Workshop © Rosella Castello
Blackhorse Workshop Gelände

Entrance
Blackhorse Workshop
Eingang Blackhorse
Workshop

The workshop is a place for both working and learning, for everyone from independent practitioners, individual hobbyists through to sole traders and small businesses. It offers a wide range of equipment and a regular programme of classes and activities. A café-bakery and brewery are open to the public, space is offered for hire, and the workshop hosts a monthly food and maker market.

Assemble developed the concept, business plan and organisational strategy for Blackhorse Workshop, working alongside the London Borough of Waltham Forest. It was established as an independent not-for-

umfasst eine vielfältige Ausstattung sowie ein regelmäßiges Kurs- und Aktivitätenprogramm und eine öffentlich zugängliche Café-Bäckerei. Arbeitsplätze können angemietet werden, und einmal im Monat findet ein Lebensmittel- und Handwerksmarkt statt.

Assemble entwickelten das Konzept, den Businessplan und die Organisationsstrategie gemeinsam mit dem Londoner Bezirk Waltham Forest. Blackhorse Workshop ist ein unabhängiges, gemeinnütziges Unternehmen, und mit einem Sitz im Verwaltungsrat sind Assemble auch weiterhin aktiv an seiner Führung beteiligt.

profit business and Assemble continue to play an active role in the ongoing direction of the workshop as members of its governing board.

Blackhorse Workshop is an interim use supported by a long-term vision. The flexibility and simplicity of the built elements are both intended to suit its current use and to be easily moved to an alternative location. The design of the workshop is based on providing a robust and adaptable work environment, built around flexible furniture elements, which are produced using the machines within the workshop. The graphic identity – developed by Europa – aims to at-

Das temporäre Nutzungskonzept basiert auf einer langfristigen Vision. Die flexiblen und unkomplizierten Bauelemente sind an die momentane Nutzung angepasst, können aber auch problemlos an einen anderen Standort übersiedelt werden. Das Design fußt auf dem Gedanken einer robusten und anpassungsfähigen Arbeitsumgebung mit flexiblen Einrichtungselementen, die mithilfe der werkstatteigenen Maschinen produziert werden. Die grafische Gestaltung des Ateliers Europa will einen großen Kreis von potenziellen Nutzer*innen ansprechen, auch Personen, die normalerweise nicht in Werkstätten arbeiten würden.

tract a wide range of people to the workshop including those who would not normally ever use one.

Assemble are working together with other open-access workshops in the UK with the aim of building a network that makes the workshop just as a familiar part of our city as libraries or leisure centres.

The project was supported by the Greater London Authority, funded by the London Borough of Waltham Forest and match-funded by Create London.

www.blackhorseworkshop.co.uk

Graphic design by Europa
Grafische Gestaltung von Europa

Zusammen mit ähnlichen Einrichtungen in Großbritannien arbeiten Assemble am Aufbau eines Netzwerks, das offene Werkstätten zu einem ebenso selbstverständlichen Bestandteil der Stadtkultur machen soll wie Bibliotheken oder Freizeitzentren.

Das Projekt erhielt Unterstützung von der Greater London Authority; die Finanzierung erfolgte durch den London Borough of Waltham Forest mit Kofinanzierung durch Create London.

FERMENTARIUM

BAKERY

Cappucino £1.50
Tea £1
Water - FREE

FENTIMANS
- CURIOSITY COLA £2
- MANDARIN AND SEVILLE ORANGE JIGGER £2
- DANDELION AND BURDOCK £2
- GINGER BEER £2

Butternut Squash & sweet potato soup £3.50

Almond cake £1

BREAD
- GOLDEN LINSEED RYE SOURDOUGH £2.10

Walthamstow, London | 67

View from the cafe into the workshop
Blick vom Café in die Werkstatt

Construction of walls
made from rubble-filled bags
Konstruktion der Wände aus mit
Bauschutt gefüllten Säcken

OTO Projects

OTOProjects is a workshop and performance space for the experimental music venue Cafe OTO in Dalston, Hackney. The building occupies a formerly disused site, granted to Cafe OTO by the council for 10 years. It is a simple single volume made using demolition waste found on the site: an informal and low-cost space for experiential and educational performance.

OTOProjects is an experiment in establishing a new material vernacular. Like the traditional London-stock brick of the

OTOProjects bietet Raum für Workshops und experimentelle Musikperformances in Dalston, Hackney (London). Das Gebäude steht auf einer Brache, die dem Auftraggeber, Cafe OTO, für zehn Jahre von der Stadtverwaltung überlassen wurde. Errichtet wurde der informelle und kostengünstige Baukörper aus dem auf dem Gelände vorgefundenen Bauschutt, was zu einem Experiment mit einer neuen Materialsprache führte.

So wie Londons Bausubstanz des 19. Jahrhunderts traditionell auf der Verwendung von Ziegeln beruht, setzte die Konstruktion von OTOProjects auf Ressourcen, die billig oder kostenlos vor Ort vorhanden sind.

Site / Ort:
Dalston, Hackney London
Year / Jahr:
2013
Client / Auftraggeber:
Cafe OTO

OTO Projects is a simple single volume made using demolition waste found on the site: an informal and low-cost space for experiential and educational performance.

Materialien wie Erde, Schutt und Kies wurden gesammelt, gesiebt, in Säcke gefüllt und verdichtet – womit aus Abfall großformatige Bausteine entstanden. Die dicken Schuttsackwände wurden mit einem dekorativen Rauputz aus Schuttmaterial versehen und mit einer leichtgewichtigen Fachwerkkonstruktion aus Holz überdacht.

An der Errichtung arbeiteten im Sommer 2013 60 Freiwillige – viele von ihnen Musiker*innen und Mitglieder von OTO. Das Projekt wurde durch Cafe OTO finanziert und erhielt Unterstützung vom Barbican Centre.

nineteenth century, the construction method is based on utilising resources that are readily available locally at little or no material cost.

The earth, rubble, and gravel on the otherwise empty site was gathered, sieved, bagged, and compressed: transformed from waste into giant building blocks. Deep rubble walls were finished with a decorative 'rubble-dash' render and topped with a lightweight timber trussed roof.

OTOProjects was built by 60 volunteers – including many musicians and OTO members – over the summer of 2013. It was supported by Cafe OTO and delivered in association with the Barbican.

The walls were finished with 'rubble-dash'.
Die Fassade wurde mit Rauputz aus Schuttmaterial versehen.

72 | **OTO Projects**

Dalston, Hackney London | 73

The wall mounting with rubble-filled
bags is visible from the inside.
Im Inneren erkennt man den Wandaufbau
aus mit Schutt gefüllten Säcken.
© Dawid Laskowski

74 | **Granby Four Streets**

Renovated street of houses
Renovierter Straßenzug

Granby
Four Streets

Granby Street was once a lively high street at the centre of one of Liverpool's most diverse communities. The demolition of all but four of Granby's streets of Victorian terraces during decades of 'regeneration' initiatives saw a once thriving community scattered, and left the remaining 'Granby Four Streets' sparsely populated and filled with tinned up houses.

Site / Ort:
Granby, Liverpool

Year / Jahr:
2014–Ongoing

Client / Auftraggeber:
Granby Four Streets
Community Land Trust

Die Granby Street war einst eine lebhafte Hauptstraße im Herzen eines Stadtteils von Liverpool, der von großer Diversität gekennzeichnet war. Im Zuge jahrzehntelanger „Erneuerungsfeldzüge" vonseiten der Stadtverwaltung wurde ein Großteil der viktorianischen Reihenhaussiedlungen abgerissen. Zurück blieben nur vier spärlich besiedelte und zu einem Gutteil mit Brettern vernagelte Straßenzüge, die dem Projekt „Granby Four Streets" seinen Namen gaben.

Einer findigen, kreativen Gruppe von Bewohner*innen ist es zu verdanken, dass diese Straßenzüge mit neuem Leben erfüllt werden. Mehr als zwei Jahrzehnte lang wurde

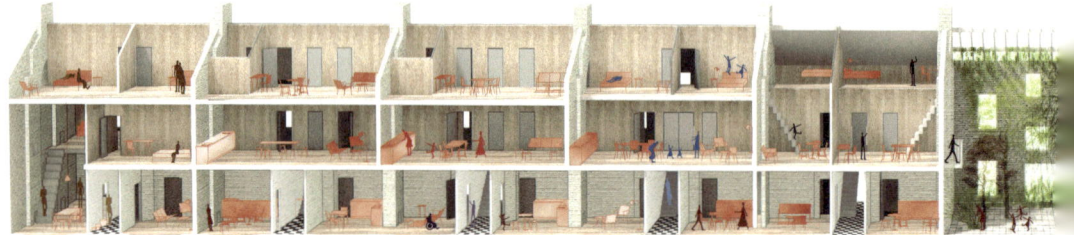

Granby Four Streets

Granby, Liverpool | 77

Elevation respectively long section through the terraced houses on Ducie street showing alternative arrangements to provide a variety of different types of living spaces.
Ansicht bzw. Schnitt durch die Reihenhäuser in der Ducie Street, der die unterschiedlichen Typen von Wohnräumen aufzeigt.

Granby Four Streets is a strategic vision that seeks to build on the extraordinary efforts of the local residents by working with them toward the sustainable and incremental improvement of the area.

The resourceful, creative actions of a group of residents were fundamental to finally bringing these streets out of dereliction and back into use. Over two decades they cleared, planted, painted, and campaigned in order to reclaim their streets. They formed the Granby Four Streets Community Land Trust in 2011 with the intention of bringing empty homes back into use as affordable housing.

Assemble worked with the Granby Four Streets CLT and the social investor Steinbeck Studios to develop an incremental approach for rebuilding the area that builds on the hard work already done by local residents and

geräumt und geplant, neu gestrichen und Öffentlichkeitsarbeit betrieben. Im Jahr 2011 gründeten die Bewohner*innen den Granby Four Streets Community Land Trust (CLT) mit dem Ziel, leer stehende Häuser in leistbaren Wohnraum zu verwandeln.

In Zusammenarbeit mit Granby Four Streets CLT und dem Sozialinvestor Steinbeck Studio entwickelten Assemble ein Konzept zur schrittweisen Wiederbelebung dieses Gebiets. Aufbauend auf der erfolgreichen Vorarbeit der Bewohner*innen werden Wohnhäuser und öffentliche Räume neu gestaltet und Beschäftigungsmöglichkeiten geschaffen.

Living space
Wohnraum

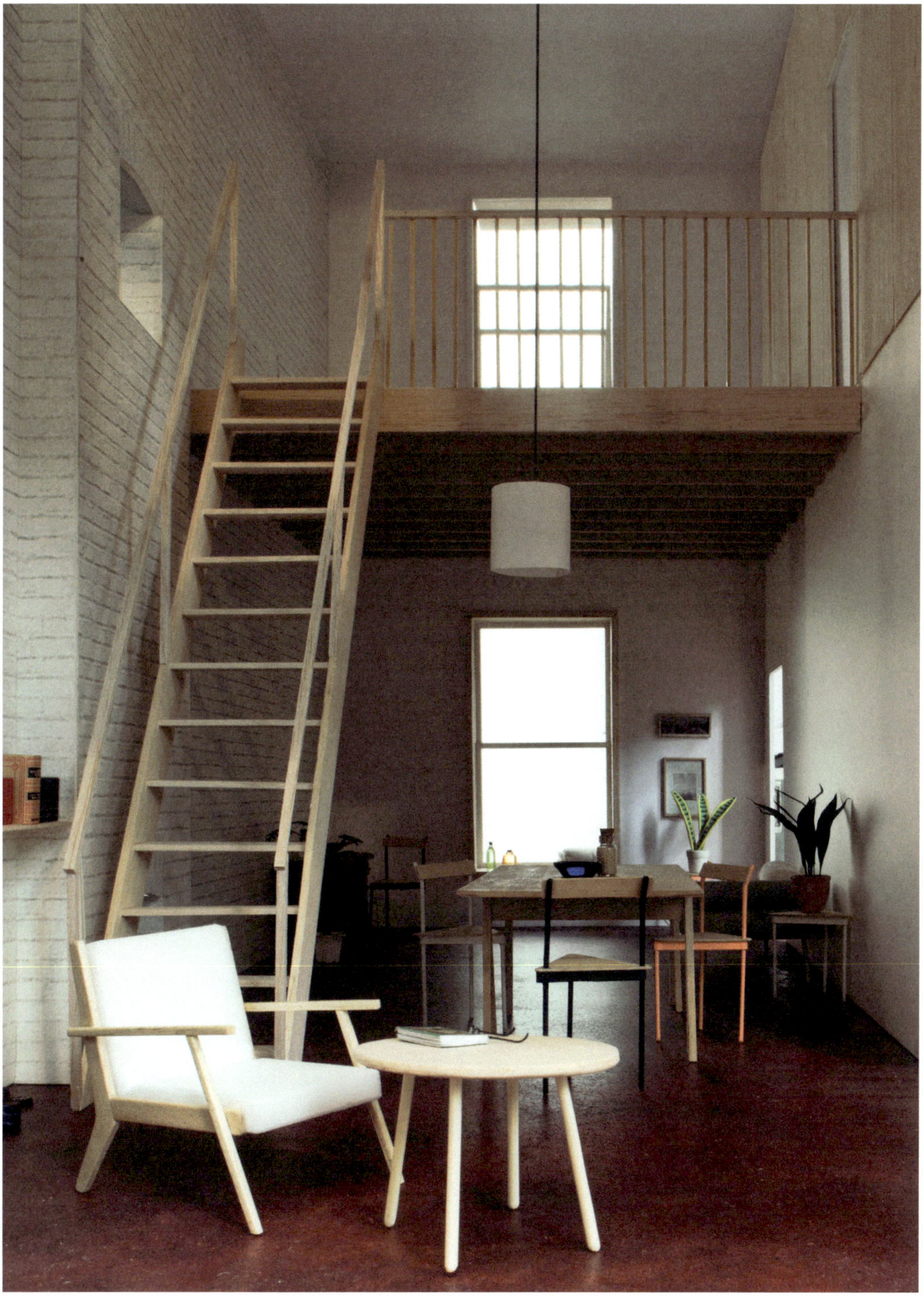

Renovation works
Renovierungsarbeiten

translates it to the refurbishment of housing, public space, and the provision of new employment opportunities.

This began with the refurbishment of 10 houses in 2014. Half are socially rented and half are for sale, using an innovative ownership model developed by the CLT keeps house prices below market value, permanently linked to the average wage in Liverpool.

Working with a modest budget, the renovation of the houses used simple methods of construction and an economic material palette. The finer details were developed on-site, in response to the differing condition of each house - leaving vaulted spaces where

Im Jahr 2014 wurde mit der Renovierung von zehn Häusern begonnen. Eine Hälfte wird als Sozialwohnungen vermietet, die andere Hälfte auf Basis eines innovativen, von CLT entwickelten Eigentumsmodells zum Kauf angeboten. Die Häuserpreise liegen unter dem Marktwert und orientieren sich am Durchschnittslohnniveau in Liverpool.

Das bescheidene Budget bedingte unkomplizierte Konstruktionsmethoden und günstige Baumaterialien für die Renovierung. Individuelle Lösungen wurden abhängig vom jeweiligen Zustand der Häuser vor Ort festgelegt. Eine eingestürzte Decke führte beispielsweise zu einem hohen Raum mit

Terrazzo fireplaces are fitted on site.
Die Terrazzo-Kamine wurden direkt vor Ort eingepasst.

ceilings had fallen through and retaining adaptations made by previous residents. Each house includes a number of playful, handmade architectural elements that replace items that had been stripped out of the houses when they were boarded up by the council. Mantelpieces, tiles, handles, and kitchen worktops, these products formed the basis for the establishment of Granby Workshop in 2015.

Dachgewölbe, aber auch die von ehemaligen Bewohner*innen vorgenommenen Eingriffe in die Bausubstanz wurden beibehalten. Für jedes Haus wurden in Handarbeit Elemente hergestellt, um architektonische Details zu ersetzen, die der Räumung durch die Stadtverwaltung zum Opfer gefallen waren. Zur Produktion dieser Elemente, darunter Kaminsimse, Fliesen, Griffe und Küchenarbeitsplatten, wurde 2015 eine eigene Werkstatt, der Granby Workshop, eingerichtet.

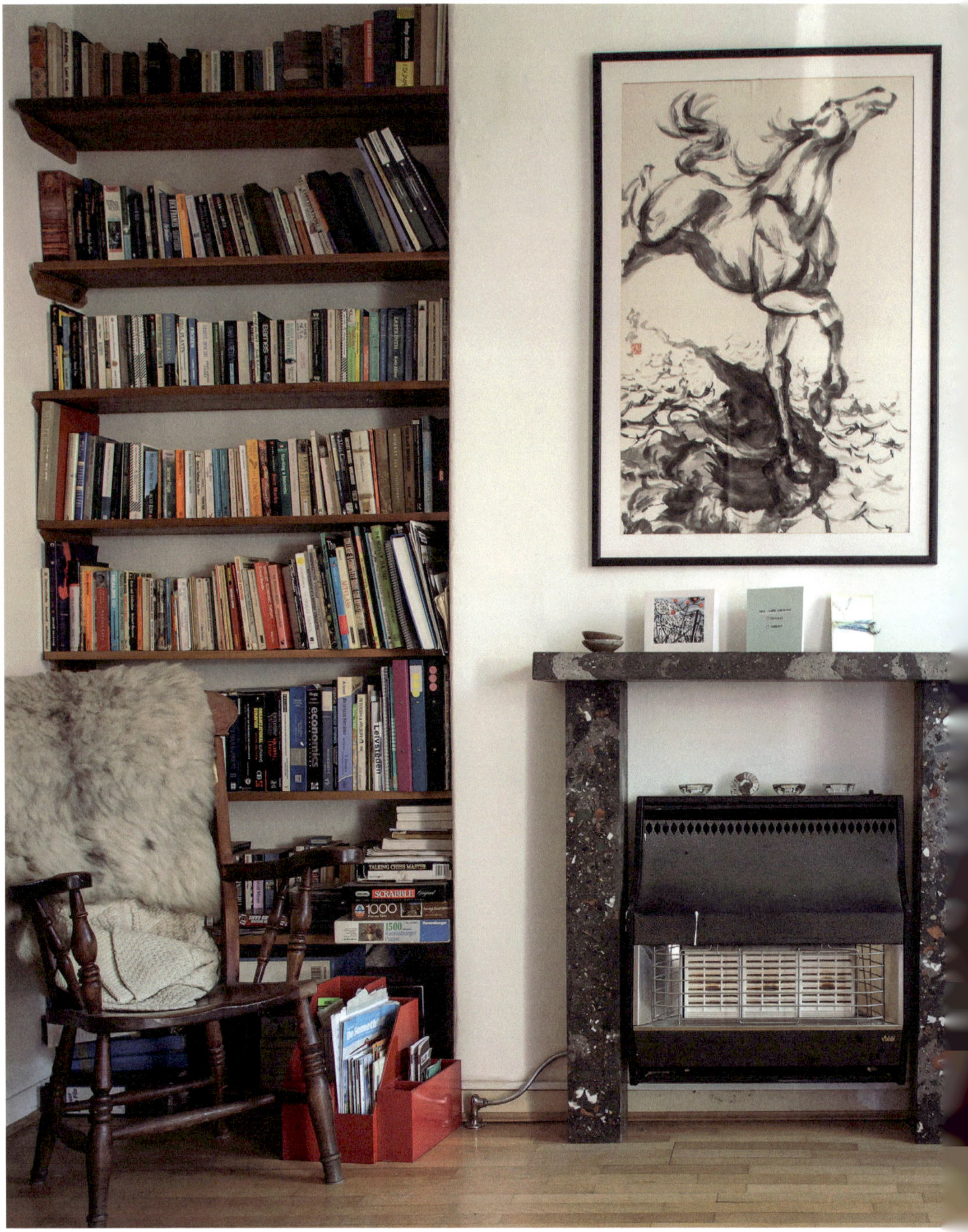

Granby, Liverpool | 83

Finished fireplace in CLT
member Eleanor's home
Kamin im Haus des
CLT-Mitglieds Eleanor

Set of goods produced
in the Granby Workshop
Produktpalette, die im Granby
Workshop hergestellt wird

Granby Workshop

Granby Workshop is a business that develops and produces experimental ceramic products and architectural materials. Launched through the Turner Prize Exhibition it was established in 2015 by Assemble, working alongside the Granby Four Streets Community Land Trust as a part of their efforts to rebuild the neighborhood.

The first range of products were a set of handmade features designed for refurbished homes in Granby and new products continue

Granby Workshop entwickelt und produziert experimentelle Keramikprodukte und andere Ausstattungsobjekte. Der von Assemble im Zuge der Turner-Prize-Ausstellung 2015 lancierte Betrieb ist Teil ihres Engagements zur Erneuerung des Liverpooler Stadtteils Granby in Zusammenarbeit mit dem Granby Four Streets Community Land Trust.

Bei den ersten Produkten handelte es sich um handgefertigte Designobjekte für die renovierten Häuser in Granby. Im Zuge der Revitalisierungsaktivitäten in einem größeren Umkreis werden aber ständig neue Produkte entwickelt. Für das Stadtviertel

Site/Ort:
Granby, Liverpool

Year/Jahr:
2015–Ongoing

Client/Auftraggeber:
Self-initiated

> **_The Workshop's products are developed through ongoing material investigations, exploring new ways of making that can uncover beauty in unlikely materials._**

to be developed in relation to the rebuilding of the wider area. The workshop is both a local employer and a resource, set up as a means of continuing to support the kind of creative, hands on activity that has brought about such immense change in the area.

The Workshop's products are developed through ongoing material investigations, exploring new ways of making that can uncover beauty in unlikely materials and give a new perspective on the materiality of our built environment. Mantelpieces are made from recycled building rubble, ceramic door handles are smoked in a domestic BBQ and fabrics are produced by block-printing offcuts of timber.

Granby ist der Workshop Arbeitgeber und Ressource zugleich. Der Betrieb wurde gegründet, um die kreativen, praxisnahen Aktivitäten weiterzuführen, die in diesem Gebiet bereits so tief greifende Veränderungen herbeigeführt haben.

Die permanente Auseinandersetzung mit Werkstoffen bestimmt die Entwicklung neuer Produkte. Es geht um neue Wege, die versteckte Schönheit unscheinbarer Materialien herauszuarbeiten und neue Perspektiven auf die Materialität unserer gebauten Umgebung zu eröffnen. Kaminsimse aus recyceltem Bauschutt, Keramiktürgriffe, die in einem Gartengrill geräuchert werden, und Textilien,

The workshop explores the creative possibilities of manufacturing, using experimental processes to introduce chance and variety to the production line so that no two products are ever the same. All products are made in Liverpool, in house and in collaboration with other local businesses.

die im Blockdruckverfahren mit Schablonen aus Holzabfällen bedruckt werden.

Das Unternehmen lotet die kreativen Möglichkeiten im Herstellungsprozess aus und experimentiert mit verschiedensten Verfahren, um Zufall und Vielfalt in die Produktion einzubauen und damit zu erreichen, dass alle Erzeugnisse Einzelstücke sind. Alle Produkte werden direkt vor Ort in Liverpool erzeugt, in Eigenproduktion oder auch in Zusammenarbeit mit ortsansässigen Betrieben.

Granby Workshop
Granby Werkstatt

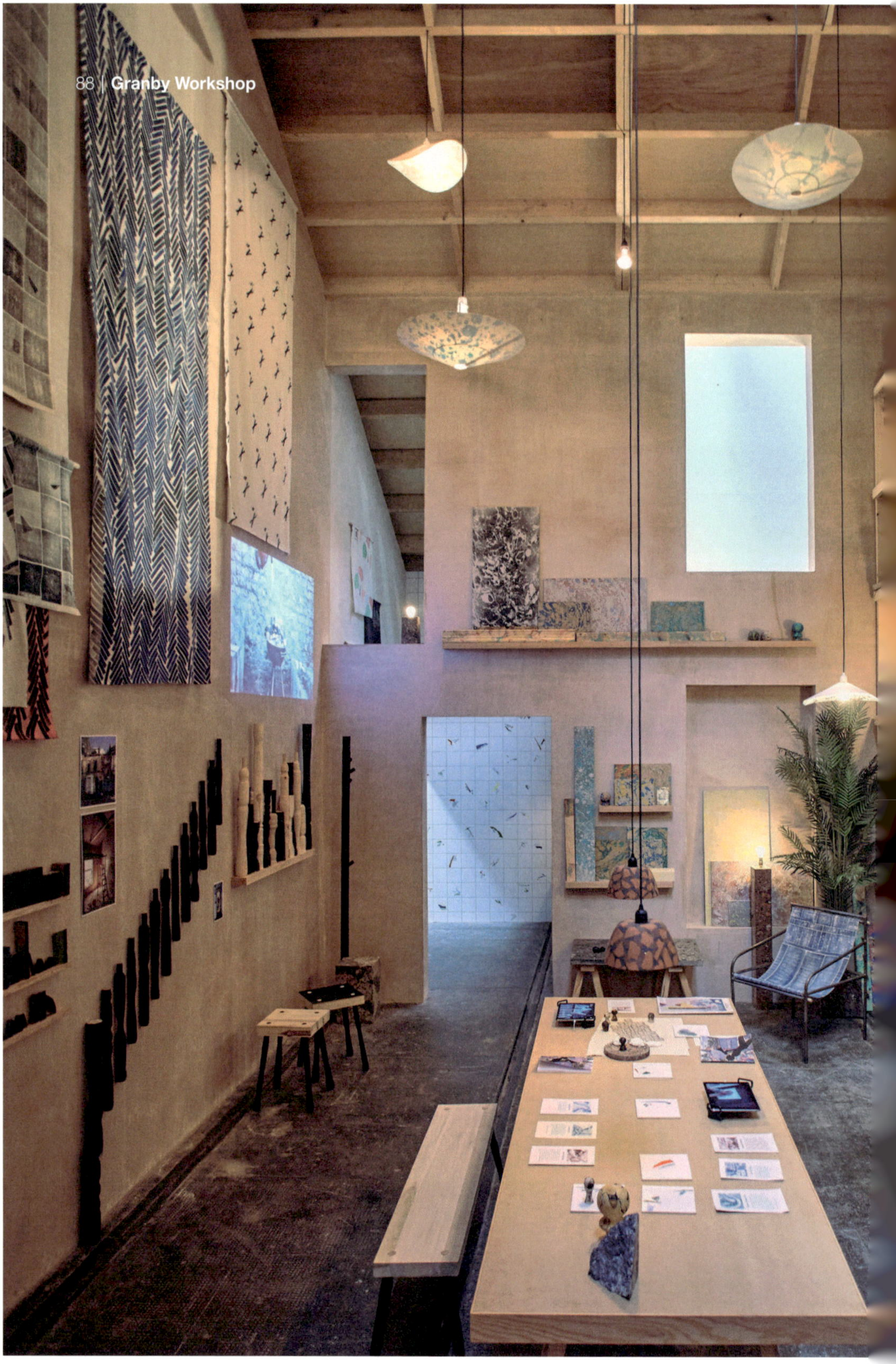

Granby, Liverpool | 89

Mould Mountain
Verschiedene Gussformen

View into the
Turner Prize Exhibition
Einblick in die Turner-Preis-
Ausstellung

View of the delerict state
of the terraced houses
Ansicht des Verfallszustandes
der Reihenhäuser

Granby Winter Garden

The Granby Winter Garden transforms two derelict terraced houses in Granby into an internal garden, meeting room, and residency space owned by and operated for the local community.

The project was developed in response to uncovering two adjacent houses in extremely poor condition, no longer possible to cost-effectively refurbish as homes. In this derelict state, these hollowed brick shells presented a completely different way

Site / Ort:
Granby, Liverpool
Year / Jahr:
2016 – Ongoing
Client / Auftraggeber:
Granby CLT

Das Projekt Granby Winter Garden verwandelt zwei verfallene Reihenhäuser in einen Innenhofgarten samt Versammlungsraum und Gästebereich. Das neu entstehende Gebäude wird im Besitz der örtlichen Bewohner*innengemeinschaft verbleiben und von ihr erhalten werden.

Der Ausgangspunkt waren zwei aneinandergrenzende Häuser in extrem schlechtem Zustand, deren Renovierung unökonomisch gewesen wäre. In diesem Verfallszustand offenbarten die ausgehöhlten Reihenhäuser jedoch eine komplett neue Sicht auf einen reizvollen Innenhof, der eine Vielzahl an potenziellen Verwendungsmöglichkeiten bietet.

The Granby Winter Garden transforms two derelict terraced houses in Granby into an internal garden, meeting room, and residency space.

of seeing the inside of a terraced house – a dramatic internal courtyard that could host a range of uses.

The Winter Garden retains the spatial drama of these found spaces, and inserts a number of facilities within them – kitchen, meeting room, work space, and residency space. The project has been made possible through support from the Arts Council and alongside its day-to-day use as a community space it will provide an ongoing artists residency programme

The project forms part of the Granby Four Streets Community Land Trust's long-term ambition to revitalise their neighbourhood.

Der Wintergarten nutzt die spannende Konstellation dieser vorgefundenen Räume und erweitert sie um eine Reihe von Einrichtungen – Küche, Versammlungsraum, Arbeits- und Gastbereich. Ermöglicht wurde das Projekt durch finanzielle Unterstützung vonseiten des Arts Council, da es neben der täglichen Nutzung als Gemeinschaftsort auch einem Artist-in-Residence-Programm zur Verfügung stehen wird.

Das Projekt reiht sich in die langfristigen Pläne des Granby Four Streets Community Land Trust (CLT) zur Revitalisierung dieses Stadtviertels ein. Der CLT ist selbst ein Ergebnis der jahrzehntelangen Bemühungen

Granby Winter Garden model in
front of the houses that will be transformed
*Granby Winter Garden Modell vor den
Häusern, die transformiert werden*

The CLT itself grew out of the residents' decades-long campaign to re-build their community through creative action, growing, and collaboration. The Winter Garden is key to ensuring that that spirit and those activities remain at the core of the area as it continues to develop and grow.

der Anwohner*innen, ihr näheres städtisches Umfeld mit kreativen Aktionen, räumlichen Erweiterungen und kollaborativen Projekten neu zu gestalten. Der Wintergarten ist ein Schlüsselelement in diesem Zusammenhang und stellt sicher, dass diese Geisteshaltung mit allen daraus erwachsenden Aktivitäten im Herzen dieses sich ständig entwickelnden Gebiets verwurzelt bleibt.

94 | Granby Winter Garden

Granby, Liverpool | 95

Conceptual image
of the Winter Garden
Visualisierung des
Wintergartens

Playing on materials found on site
Spielen mit den vor
Ort gefundenen Materialien

Baltic Street Adventure Playground

Baltic Street Adventure Playground is a playground and organisation in Dalmarnock, East Glasgow, realised through an on-going collaboration with the children and families of Dalmarnock and a growing group of many others. The project was proposed in response to an open public art commission for the 2014 Commonwealth Games. It was initiated as an immediate, practical response to the challenges facing a group of children

Site / Ort:
Dalmarnock, East Glasgow
Year / Jahr:
2013
Client / Auftraggeber:
Velocity, Creative Scotland, Clyde Gateway & The 2014 Commonwealth Games

Baltic Street Adventure Playground ist ein Abenteuerspielplatz und der Name einer damit in Zusammenhang stehenden Organisation im Glasgower Stadtteil Dalmarnock. Realisiert wurde das Projekt in enger Zusammenarbeit mit den Kindern von Dalmarnock, ihren Familien und einer wachsenden Gruppe von Interessent*innen. Das Projekt wurde initiiert als unmittelbare und konkrete Antwort auf die Herausforderungen des täglichen Lebens in einer relativ kargen urbanen Umgebung, in der etwa 54 % der Familien unterhalb der Armutsgrenze leben.

Als Inspiration dienten die nach dem Krieg in England etablierten Abenteuer-

'Better a broken bone than a broken spirit'

growing up in a relatively scarce urban environment where around 54% of children live below the poverty line.

Drawing inspiration from the post-war junk playground and Lady Allen's 1950s mantra, 'better a broken bone than a broken spirit', Baltic Street is a supervised child-led space offering free open-access play, caring adults, daily campfire food, and warm and waterproof clothes to children from 6 to 12 years of age. Based on the understanding that, as Hakim Bey put it, "cherishing and unleashing are the same act", Baltic Street offers space for children to grow in every and any direction they choose, embracing

spielplätze und das Mantra der Landschaftsarchitektin und Kinderfreundin Lady Allen aus den 1950ern: „Lieber gebrochene Knochen als ein gebrochener Geist." Baltic Street ist ein frei zugänglicher Ort, den Kinder im Alter von 6 bis 12 Jahren nach ihren Vorstellungen gestalten können. Sie finden dort erwachsene Betreuer*innen, tägliches Essen am Lagerfeuer und warme, wasserfeste Kleidung. Frei nach dem Grundsatz von Hakim Bey, „lieben heißt freilassen", bietet Baltic Street den Kindern Raum, um in jeder Hinsicht zu wachsen und kreative, aber auch destruktive Impulse auszuleben. Die Kinder werden dazu ermutigt, selbstbestimmt zu

Dalmarnock, East Glasgow | 99

Playing between the trees on site
Spielwiese zwischen Bäumen

Children are creating
their playing environment
Kinder schaffen sich ihre
Spielumgebung selbst

both creativity and destruction. Children are supported to self-organise, and playworkers maintain a secure, nurturing environment, which is constantly evolving on a moment-to-moment and month-to-month basis in response to the children's growing needs, dreams, and capacity to affect change.

Baltic Street argues for the continued relevance of the adventure playground as a counterpoint to the pressures of modern urban childhood, believing they are still a refuge of a delightfully simple but powerful set of ideas about both childhood and our relationship to our immediate environment.

entscheiden, wobei die Spielbetreuer*innen für eine sichere, anregende Umgebung sorgen. Der Spielplatz verändert und entwickelt sich unablässig als Ergebnis der Bedürfnisse, Wünsche und Aktionen der Kinder.

Baltic Street ist ein Plädoyer für die ungebrochene Relevanz von Abenteuerspielplätzen. Sie setzen einen Kontrapunkt zu den begrenzten Möglichkeiten einer Kindheit in der Stadt von heute und schaffen Raum für ein paar einfache, aber wirkmächtige Vorstellungen zum Thema Kindheit in Bezug auf unsere unmittelbare Umgebung.

Baltic Street war ein Auftrag im Bereich Kunst im öffentlichen Raum in Vorberei-

Playworkers maintain a secure and nurturing environment
Spielbetreuer*innen sorgen für eine sichere und angenehme Umgebung

Baltic Street was the lead public art commission for the 2014 Commonwealth Games, funded by Velocity, produced by Create and supported by Creative Scotland, Clyde Gateway, and the Commonwealth Games.

tung auf die Commonwealth Games in Glasgow 2014. Die Finanzierung erfolgte durch Velocity, die Errichtung durch Create mit Unterstützung von Creative Scotland, Clyde Gateway und Commonwealth Games.

| 02 | Baltic Street Adventure Playground

Dalmarnock, East Glasgow | 103

104 | **Goldsmiths Art Gallery**

Conceptual image
of Goldsmiths Art Gallery
Visualisierung der
Goldsmiths Art Gallery

Goldsmiths Art Gallery

Assemble are working with Goldsmiths University to transform a series of historic, listed, and infrastructural spaces into a new public art gallery, a site for an active public conversation around contemporary art practice.

The new gallery will be built out of a network of existing spaces within the former Victorian bathhouse at Laurie Grove, to create an ensemble of distinct rooms, offering flexibility through their variety. Many of the

Im Auftrag der Goldsmiths University planen Assemble den Umbau einer Reihe von historischen, denkmalgeschützten Räumen in eine neue öffentliche Kunstgalerie, einen Ort der aktiven öffentlichen Auseinandersetzung mit zeitgenössischer Kunst.

Die neue Galerie entsteht aus einem Netzwerk von bestehenden Räumen in einem früheren viktorianischen Badehaus am Laurie Grove. Ziel des Umbaus ist ein Zusammenspiel von individuellen Raumkategorien mit vielfältigen Verwendungsmöglichkeiten. Etliche der gusseisernen Wassertanks des Badehauses können erhalten bleiben, während neue Galerieräume

Site / Ort:
Goldsmiths Campus, Lewisham, London
Year / Jahr:
2014 – Ongoing
Client / Auftraggeber:
Goldsmiths, University of London

Assemble are going to transform a series of historic, listed and infrastructural spaces into a new public art gallery.

bath's cast-iron water tanks will be preserved, whilst new top-lit galleries will be inserted to provide a distinct spatial counterpoint.

Central to the proposal is the double-height project space, formed by cutting a void in the existing floor plate. By putting an active project space at the heart of the building, the scheme prioritises openness and making opportunities for a wider public to engage in an ongoing conversation of contemporary art practice.

Goldsmiths Gallery was commissioned by Goldsmiths, University of London. Assemble were appointed to the project after winning an open design competition in 2014.

mit Oberlicht einen spannungsreichen räumlichen Kontrapunkt setzen.

Ein wesentliches Entwurfselement ist der doppelgeschossige Projektraum, der durch Entfernen eines Teils der Deckenplatte entsteht. Seine Positionierung im Zentrum des Gebäudes entspricht dem Konzept der Öffnung und bietet vielfältige Möglichkeiten, ein größeres Publikum in die Auseinandersetzung mit aktueller Kunstpraxis einzubinden.

Der Auftrag für die Gestaltung der Goldsmiths Art Gallery wurde von Goldsmiths, University of London vergeben. Assemble gewannen den offenen Designwettbewerb im Jahr 2014.

Goldsmiths Campus, Lewisham, London | 107

1:1 facade test made from cement board
1:1 Test der Fassade aus Zementplatten

Sectional model
showing the number of different spaces
carved from the existing building.
Das Schnittmodell zeigt die unterschiedlichen
Räume, die in das bestehende Gebäude
eingeschnitten werden.

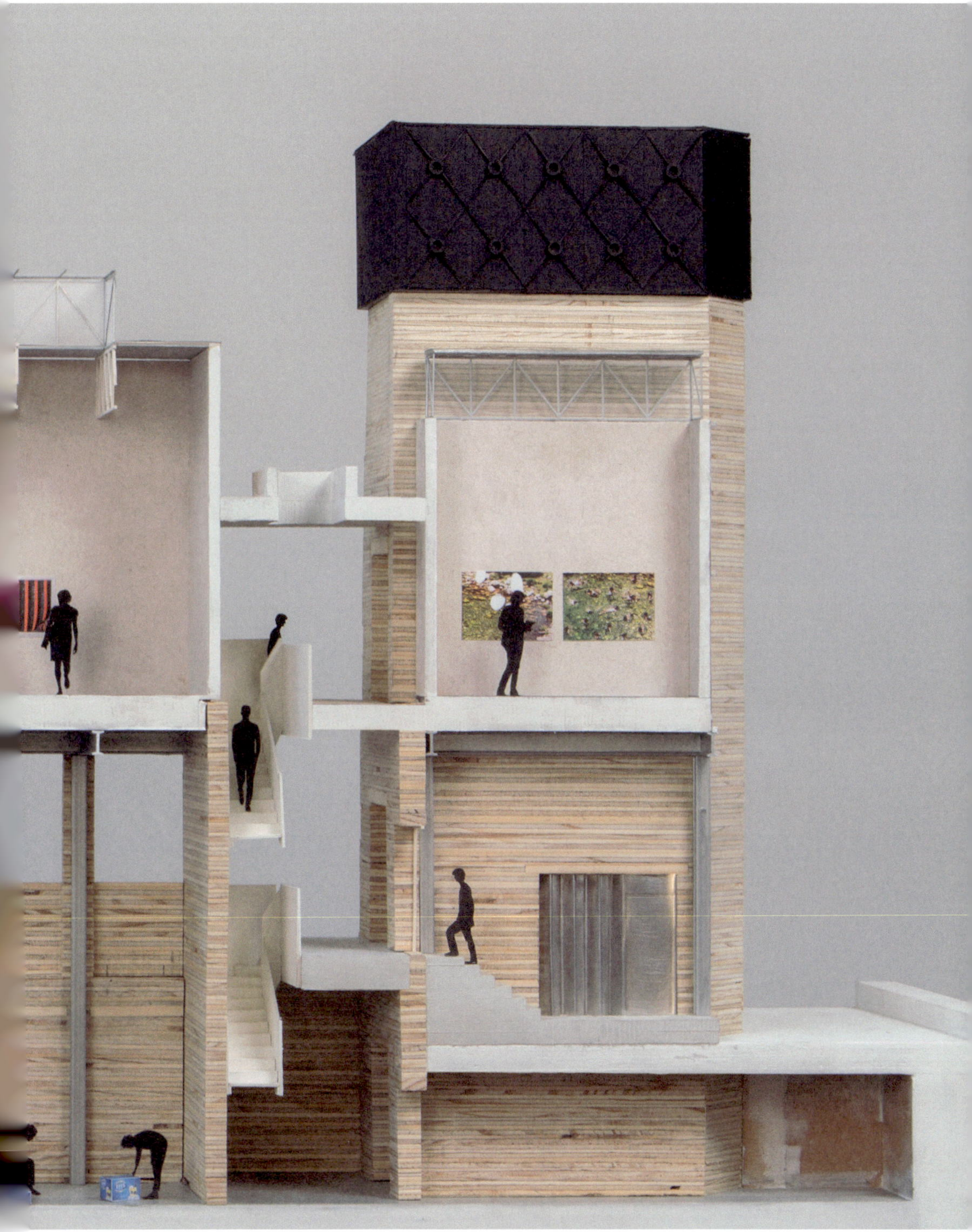

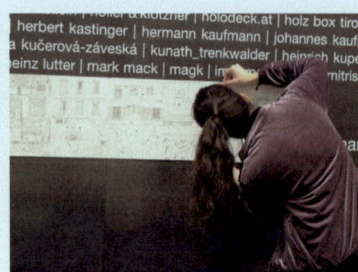

How we Build

*Assemble visiting professorship at the
TU Wien in collaboration with David Calas*

The studio was founded on the belief that an understanding of how things are made, of how materials are assembled, brings an intimate engagement with the problems and possibilities of the real world.

The studio was split across two semesters. The first semester focused on analysis and drawing, and the second prioritized hands-on material exploration and 1:1 prototyping. We began by investigating a range of buildings constructed at different points in Vienna's history where specific methods of construction were employed as a reflection of social, economic, and political circumstances. These included examples of mass-housing, self-build projects, institutional buildings, places of worship, and places of work. Through detailed axonometric drawings we communicated new ways of reading the city.

Impressions of Assembles visiting professorship at the TU Wien/future.lab
Eindrücke zur Gastprofessur von Assemble an der TU Wien/future.lab
© TU Wien / Institut für Kunst und Gestaltung (p. / S. 110–126)

The second semester was a design and build project, to make a small but active public kiosk, based around the single most abundant material resource of the city: the clay under our feet. In collaboration with the Wienerberger factory in Hennersdorf, we learnt about current brick production, subsequently adapting the various stages of the process in our proposal. In partnership with Architekturzentrum Wien, the City of Vienna, future.lab, and the Institute for Art and Design, the building has been built in the MuseumsQuartier courtyard, acting as a public ceramic workshop and infrastructure for summer events.

The studio was a collective endeavor; we developed a wide body of work through individual interests and shared group focus.

We would also like to thank Gerhard Zsutty and the Brick Museum, who provided great insight and inspiration into our rich heritage of clay brick culture, and CREAU – the transitory use project from NEST for hosting us during the summer semester.

Case Study Clara Berthaud, Otto Wagner Stadtbahnstation, 2016

RINGTURM

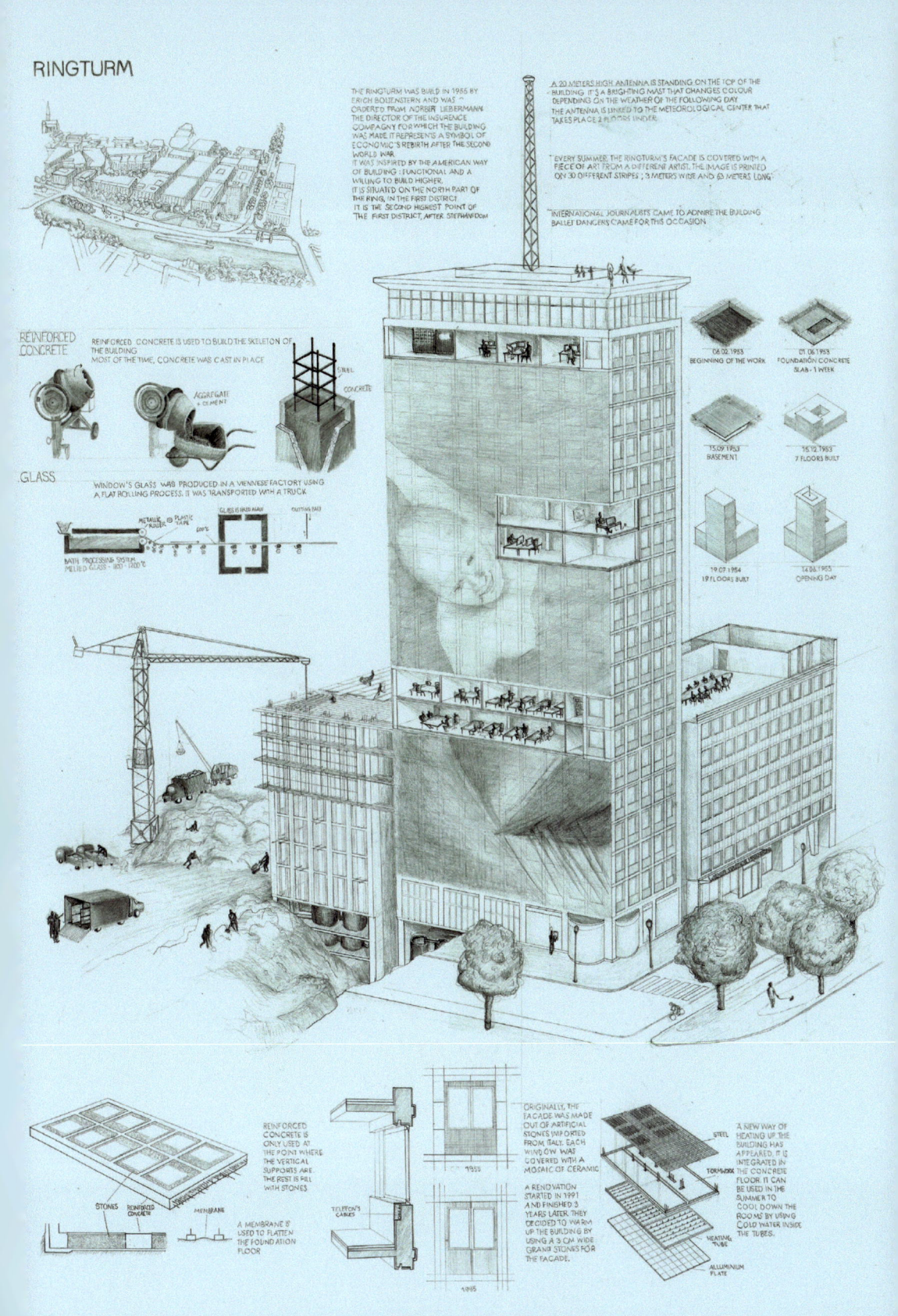

THE RINGTURM WAS BUILD IN 1955 BY ERICH BOLTENSTERN AND WAS ORDERED FROM NORBER LIEBERMANN THE DIRECTOR OF THE INSURENCE COMPAGNY FOR WHICH THE BUILDING WAS MADE. IT REPRESENTS A SYMBOL OF ECONOMIC'S REBIRTH AFTER THE SECOND WORLD WAR.
IT WAS INSPIRED BY THE AMERICAN WAY OF BUILDING : FUNCTIONAL AND A WILLING TO BUILD HIGHER.
IT IS SITUATED ON THE NORTH PART OF THE RING, IN THE FIRST DISTRICT.
IT IS THE SECOND HIGHEST POINT OF THE FIRST DISTRICT, AFTER STEPHANSDOM.

A 20 METERS HIGH ANTENNA IS STANDING ON THE TOP OF THE BUILDING. IT'S A BRIGHTING MAST THAT CHANGES COLOUR DEPENDING ON THE WEATHER OF THE FOLLOWING DAY. THE ANTENNA IS LINKED TO THE METEOROLOGICAL CENTER THAT TAKES PLACE 2 FLOORS UNDER.

EVERY SUMMER, THE RINGTURM'S FACADE IS COVERED WITH A PIECE OF ART FROM A DIFFERENT ARTIST. THE IMAGE IS PRINTED ON 30 DIFFERENT STRIPES ; 3 METERS WIDE AND 63 METERS LONG.

INTERNATIONAL JOURNALISTS CAME TO ADMIRE THE BUILDING. BALLET DANCERS CAME FOR THIS OCCASION.

REINFORCED CONCRETE

REINFORCED CONCRETE IS USED TO BUILD THE SKELETON OF THE BUILDING.
MOST OF THE TIME, CONCRETE WAS CAST IN PLACE.

GLASS

WINDOW'S GLASS WAS PRODUCED IN A VIENNESE FACTORY USING A FLAT ROLLING PROCESS. IT WAS TRANSPORTED WITH A TRUCK.

- 08.02.1953 BEGINNING OF THE WORK
- 01.06.1953 FOUNDATION CONCRETE SLAB - 1 WEEK
- 15.09.1953 BASEMENT
- 15.12.1953 7 FLOORS BUILT
- 19.07.1954 19 FLOORS BUILT
- 14.06.1955 OPENING DAY

REINFORCED CONCRETE IS ONLY USED AT THE POINT WHERE THE VERTICAL SUPPORTS ARE. THE REST IS FILL WITH STONES.

A MEMBRANE IS USED TO FLATTEN THE FOUNDATION FLOOR.

ORIGINALLY, THE FACADE WAS MADE OUT OF ARTIFICIAL STONES IMPORTED FROM ITALY. EACH WINDOW WAS COVERED WITH A MOSAIC OF CERAMIC.

A RENOVATION STARTED IN 1991 AND FINISHED 3 YEARS LATER. THEY DECIDED TO WARM UP THE BUILDING BY USING A 3 CM WIDE GRANIT STONES FOR THE FACADE.

A NEW WAY OF HEATING UP THE BUILDING HAS APPEARED. IT IS INTEGRATED IN THE CONCRETE FLOOR. IT CAN BE USED IN THE SUMMER TO COOL DOWN THE ROOMS BY USING COLD WATER INSIDE THE TUBES.

Case Study Valentine Robin, Ringturm, 2016

Wie wir bauen

*Assembles Gastprofessur an der
TU Wien in Zusammenarbeit mit David Calas*

Das Entwerfen-Studio beruht auf der Überzeugung, dass das Begreifen von „wie Dinge gemacht sind" und „wie Materialien zusammengefügt werden", eine intensive Auseinandersetzung mit den Problemen und den Möglichkeiten der realen Welt eröffnet.

Das Studio erstreckte sich über ein Studienjahr: Während das erste Semester den Schwerpunkt auf Analyse und Zeichnen legte, setzte das zweite Semester auf eine praxisnahe Auseinandersetzung mit Werkstoffen und die Errichtung eines Prototypen im Maßstab 1:1. Den Ausgangspunkt bildete die Analyse einiger Bauten aus verschiedenen Epochen in Wien, deren spezifische Baumethoden Ausdruck einer bestimmten sozialen, wirtschaftlichen und politischen Situation sind. Die Baubeispiele umfassten Wohnbauten, Selbstbauprojekte, öffentliche Gebäude, religiöse Bauten und Arbeitsstätten. Mithilfe detaillierter axonometrischer Zeichnungen wurden neue Lesarten der Stadt kommuniziert.

Wie wir bauen | 115

Im zweiten Semester lag der Schwerpunkt auf Entwerfen und Bauen, insbesondere auf der Konstruktion eines kleinen, aber aktiv zu nutzenden öffentlichen Pavillons aus jenem Grundmaterial, das für die Wiener Bauten am allerhäufigsten verwendet wurde: dem Lehm unter unseren Füßen. Bei der Wienerberger-Ziegelfabrik in Hennersdorf informierten wir uns über den heutigen Stand in der Ziegelproduktion und adaptierten die einzelnen Stufen dieses Prozesses für unser Projekt. In partnerschaftlicher Zusammenarbeit mit dem Az W, der Stadt Wien, dem future.lab und dem Institut für Kunst und Gestaltung entstand der Bau im Hof des Architekturzentrum Wien. Er dient während des Sommers als öffentlich zugängliche Keramikwerkstatt und als Veranstaltungsort.

Das Studio war ein kollektives Unterfangen; im Zusammenspiel der Einzelinteressen und mit einem gemeinsamen Gruppenschwerpunkt entwickelte sich ein umfangreicher Arbeitskorpus.

―――

Wir bedanken uns auch bei Gerhard Zsutty und dem Wiener Ziegelmuseum für wertvolle Einblicke und Inspirationen in Bezug auf das reiche Erbe der Ziegelbaukultur und bei CREAU – einem Zwischennutzungsprojekt von NEST –, die uns während des Sommersemesters Werkräume zur Verfügung gestellt haben.

In March 2017, the students got access to the CREAU premises to work on
the pavilion and conduct experiments with the material.
Im März 2017 konnten die Studierenden Räume in der CREAU beziehen, um dort
am Pavillon zu arbeiten und diverse Materialexperimente durchzuführen.

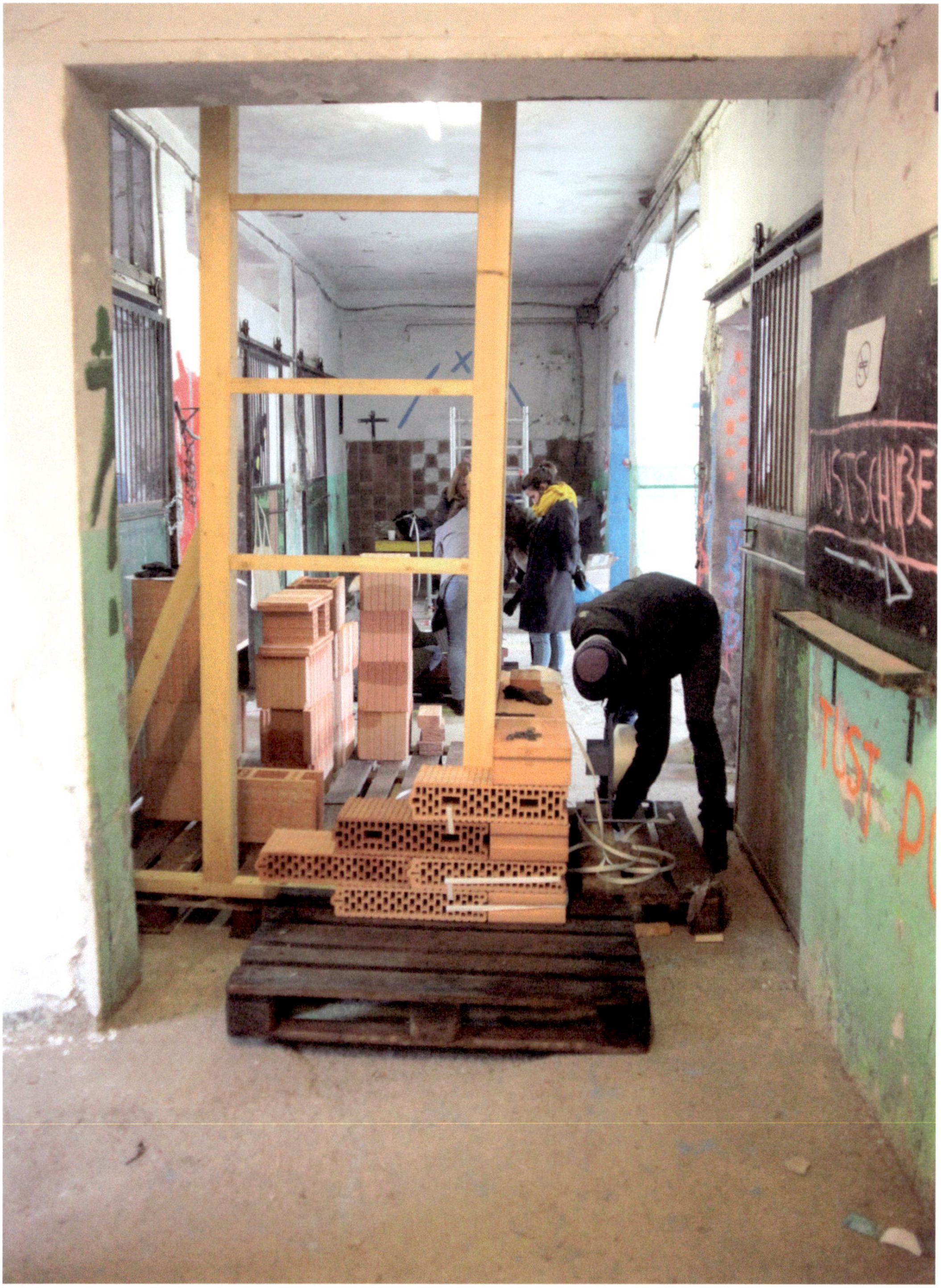

Students of the TU Wien working on the temporary
pavilion for the Architekturzentrum Wien.
Student*innen der TU Wien arbeiten am temporären
Pavillon für das Architekturzentrum Wien.

Clara Berthaud, Paula Brücke, Matthias Garzon, Christophe Gonçalves Marques,
Katharina Hummer, Katharina Jecminek, Clara Marie Linsmeier, Bernhard Mayer, Aaron Merdinger,
Thomas Musil, Patrick Olczykowski, Lana Petrovic, Charles Rauchs, Valentine Marie Robin,
Yamina Sam, Elisabeth Sellmeier, Lukas Trappl, Marija Urosevic, Marina Urosevic, Elisa Zambarda

Students co-designing the pavilion
Student*innen entwerfen gemeinsam den Pavillon

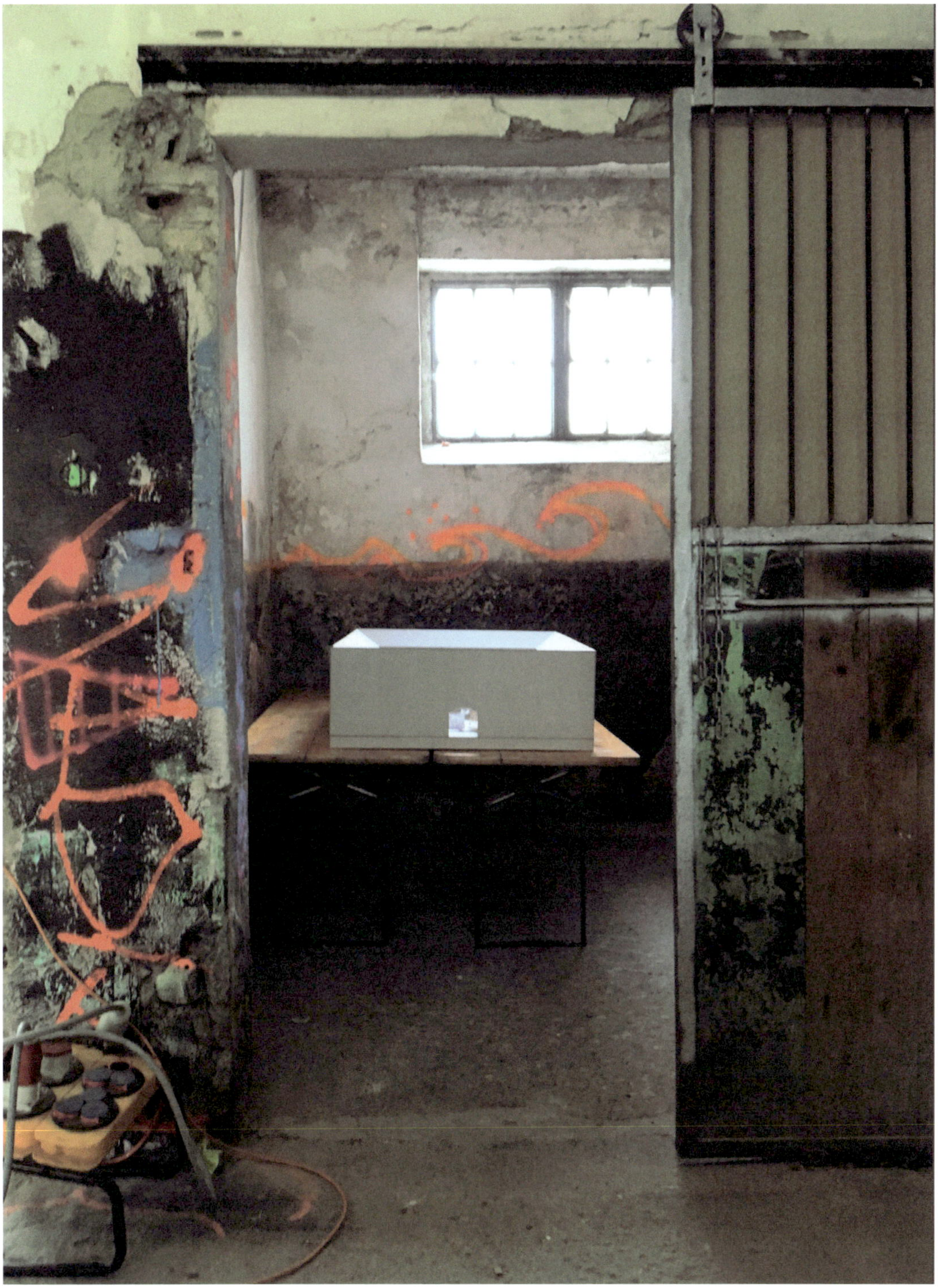

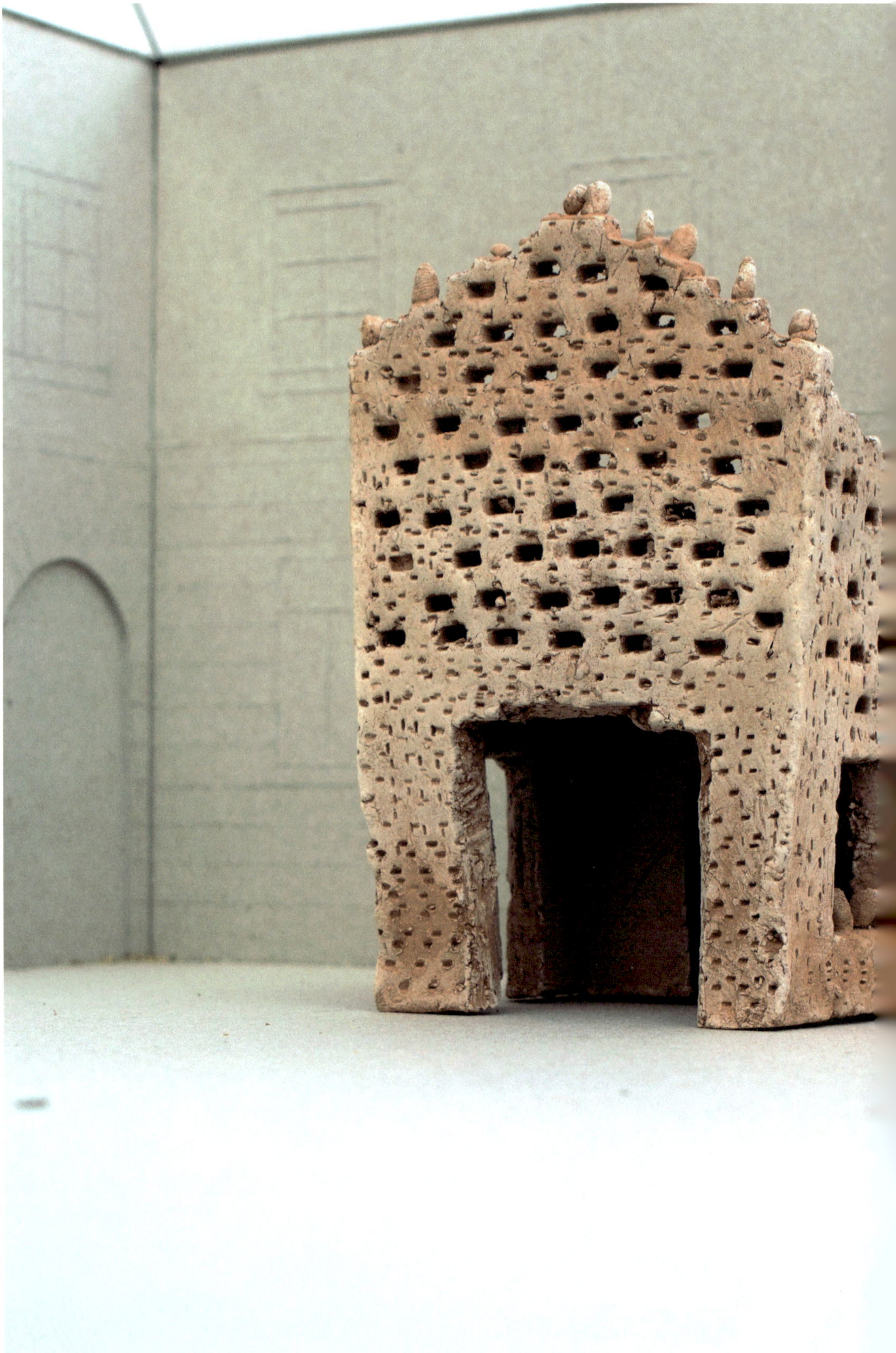

Clay model for the
pavilion in the courtyard of the
Architekturzentrum Wien
Ton-Modell für den Pavillon im Hof
des Architekturzentrum Wien

From construction model to 1:1 test
Vom Konstruktionsmodell zum 1:1 Test

Marktplatz für
Mode, Design
Kunst und
Ideen

StadtBiotop

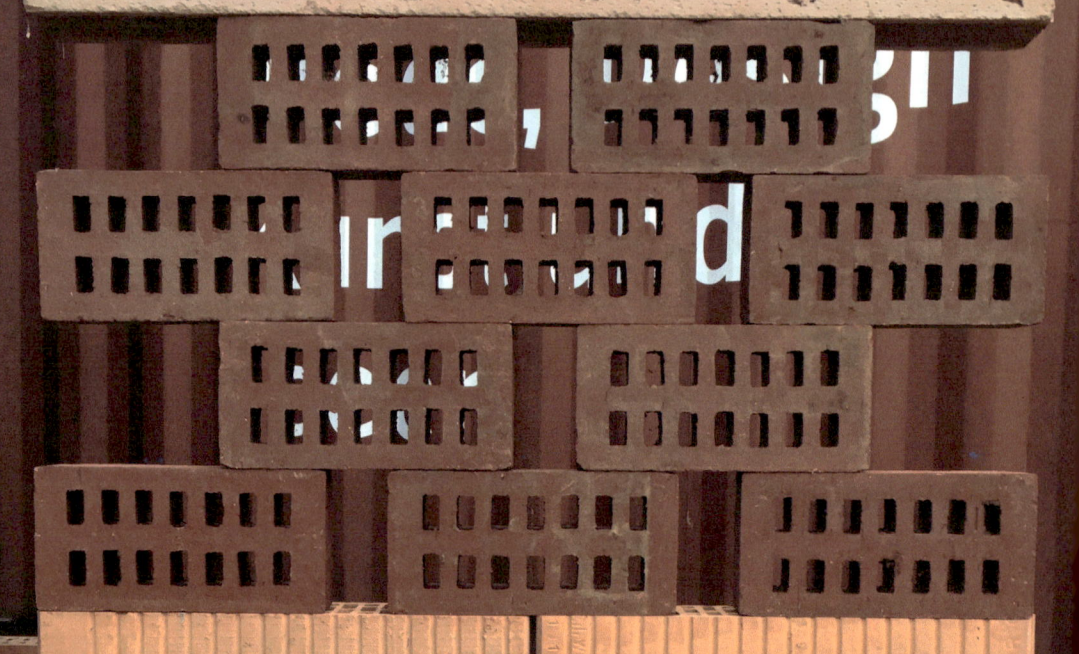

Niamh Riordan, The Stucco Paradox

The Stucco Paradox

Das Stuck-Paradox

"_Immense stucco shams_" So said American visitor Mr Henry Pettit of Vienna's World's Fair exhibition buildings in 1873. Pettit was visiting as part of a delegation from Philadelphia, a research visit for that city's own World's Fair in 1876.

He goes on: "The stucco finish admits of the most elaborate ornamentation, being introduced at small cost, and produces an effect which is wonderfully monumental, so long as one forgets that it is all a sham, and that the columns, cornices, window architraves, balustrades, vases and statuary are made of a substance but a little better than common plaster …"

„_Ungeheure Stuckschwindeleien_" – so beschrieb der amerikanische Besucher Henry Pettit die Ausstellungsgebäude der Wiener Weltausstellung 1873, die er mit einer Delegation aus Philadelphia auf Forschungsmission für die Weltausstellung im Jahr 1876 besuchte.

Er meinte weiter: „Die Stuckverkleidung ermöglicht das Anbringen von höchst kunstvoller Verzierung zu geringen Kosten und erzeugt eine wundersam monumentale Wirkung, solange man nicht daran denkt, dass alles Schein ist und dass die Säulen, Gesimse, Fensterbalken, Brüstungen, Vasen und Plastiken aus einem Stoff bestehen, der kaum besser als gewöhnlicher Gips ist ..."

Various bricks from Wienerberger
Verschiedene Wienerberger-Ziegel

In a park on the Southern edge of Vienna, Austria's only native species of turtle, the highly endangered Emis Obicularis (European Pond Turtle) flourishes in the watery remnants of what used to be the site of Vienna's brickworks. These ponds in Wienerberg park were once clay pits, which, up until the 1960s, supplied Vienna's longstanding and hugely successful brick industry. It was this local clay which made Vienna the centre of Europe's brick production, and Wienerberger the world's largest brick producer.

The Romans were the first to discover clay deposits in the region, and brick production continued throughout the centuries. By the 19th century, workers from all over the Austro-Hungarian Empire were drawn to the city seeking employment in the brickworks. The Imperial seal of the brick manufacturer became a symbol for the power and economic success of the Habsburg empire.

Vienna is largely brick built. Yet much of the city's historic architecture presents a different face to the world. Vienna may have bones of brick, but on its surface it is a city of stucco. Centuries of architectural fashions leaned towards the coating of these local

In einem Park südlich von Wien gedeiht Österreichs einzige einheimische Schildkrötenart, die hochgradig bedrohte *Emys orbicularis* (Europäische Sumpfschildkröte), in den Restgewässern des Areals der ehemaligen Wiener Ziegelwerke. Diese Tümpel im Wienerbergpark waren einst Lehmgruben, aus denen bis in die 1960er-Jahre Wiens traditionsreiche und enorm erfolgreiche Ziegelindustrie beliefert wurde. Dank dieses Lehmvorkommens wurde Wien zum Zentrum der europäischen Ziegelproduktion und Wienerberger zum weltgrößten Ziegelhersteller.

Die Römer entdeckten als erste die Lehmvorkommen dieser Gegend, und die Ziegelproduktion wurde über Jahrhunderte fortgeführt. Im 19. Jahrhundert strömten Arbeiter aus allen Ecken der Doppelmonarchie in die Stadt in der Hoffnung auf Arbeit in den Ziegelwerken. Das kaiserliche Siegel des Ziegelherstellers wurde zum Symbol der Macht und Wirtschaftsstärke des Habsburgerreichs.

Auch wenn Wien hauptsächlich aus Ziegelbauten besteht, zeigt der Großteil seiner historischen Substanz der Welt ein anderes Antlitz. Die Knochen Wiens mögen aus

Wiener Rotunde,
Vienna World's Fair, 1873
Wiener Rotunde, Weltausstellung
Wien, 1873

aus: Ulrike Felber, Carla Camilleri, Technisches Museum Wien (Hg.), Welt ausstellen. Schauplatz Wien 1873, Wien 2004

bricks in a layer of exterior plaster. From modest apartment blocks to the city's grandest buildings, the fabric of the city is hidden beneath a pale, unifying skin.

Inside one of the World's Fair 'stucco shams', Mr Pettit would have found a triumphal arch, high and broad enough for a carriage to drive through, constructed entirely of red and buff bricks, and studded with terracotta ornaments – cornices, mouldings, statues, bas-reliefs, and medallions, some plain, others brightly enamelled. Beneath this archway, an exhibition, on tables and counters, of all variety of bricks: plain, colourful, oblong, wedge shaped, rounded,

Backstein sein, aber an der Oberfläche ist es eine Stadt aus Putz. Über Jahrhunderte folgte man dem Trend, die Ziegel in eine Schicht Außenputz zu kleiden. Von bescheidenen Zinshäusern bis hin zu den Prachtbauten Wiens verbirgt sich das Stadtgefüge unterschiedslos unter einer blassen Haut.

Im Inneren der „Stuckschwindeleien" der Weltausstellung mag Henry Pettit einen Triumphbogen vorgefunden haben, hoch und breit genug, dass eine Kutsche durchfahren konnte, vollkommen aus roten und gelben Ziegeln gefertigt und mit Terrakotta-Ornamenten verziert: Gesimse, Friese, Statuen, Flachreliefs und Medaillons, einige schlicht,

curved, or moulded. A majolica wall fountain would have spouted merrily in one corner. This was the Wienerberger exhibit – a monumental display of the company's brick making expertise. Another impressed American visitor, a Mr William P. Blake, was to report "the bricks being so perfect in form and finish that, when well laid, no surface plastering or decoration is required."

A celebration of the material and decorative properties of unconcealed brick, housed inside a stucco coated confection. It is an image which foreshadows a concern with material honesty that would preoccupy architecture for the following century.

Poor man's stone

For thousands of years, we have clad our buildings in plaster renders, whether to protect, disguise, or decorate the surface beneath. The earliest plasters known to mankind were lime-based. Around 7500 BC, the people of ʿAin Ghazal in Jordan used lime mixed with unheated crushed limestone to make plaster which was used on a large

andere bunt glasiert. Unter diesem Bogen befand sich eine Ausstellung aller Arten von Backsteinen: schlichte, farbige, rechteckige, keilförmige, runde, gebogene und geformte. Ein Wandbrunnen aus Majolika plätscherte fröhlich in einer Ecke. Das war die Wienerberger-Ausstellung – eine monumentale Darbietung der Ziegelbrennkunst des Unternehmens. William P. Blake, ein beeindruckter Besucher aus Amerika, sollte berichten: „Die Backsteine waren in Form und Ausführung so vollendet, dass bei geschicktem Verlegen weder Putz noch Verzierung erforderlich ist."

Zelebriert wurden die stofflichen und schmückenden Eigenschaften von Backstein, und das in einem stuckverzierten Gebilde: Ein Bild, das als Vorgriff auf das Anliegen der Materialgerechtigkeit dienen kann, das die Architektur im folgenden Jahrhundert beschäftigen sollte.

Der Stein der armen Leute

Seit Jahrtausenden verkleiden wir unsere Gebäude mit Putz, um die Flächen darunter zu schützen, zu verbergen oder zu schmücken.

scale for covering walls, floors, and hearths in their houses. The Ancient Egyptians gave buildings intricately painted coats of lime and gypsum plaster. The Romans used lime plaster in relief to simulate monumental architecture – the first civilization to fake three dimensional architectural features – a practice which would be resurrected by Renaissance architects, who embraced molded stucco to produce fine exterior decoration.

Stucco's persistent popularity is easy to fathom. It is cheap and durable. It can be molded and shaped to suit the most fanciful of designs. Also known as the poor man's stone, it can readily imitate more expensive materials such as granite or marble, and consequently can be found in widespread use in areas (like Vienna and London) where stone quarries are distant, to give the impression of solidity and grandeur at low, low prices.

The stucco recipe is a flexible one, and has often been cooked up using a surprisingly ad-hoc range of ingredients. In 17th century England, exterior plaster might have included fruit juice, beer, blood, cheese, or beeswax. Just mix with household or bodily fluids, to achieve your desired consistency.

Die ersten Putzarten basierten auf der Verwendung von Kalk. Um 7500 v. Chr. mischte man in ʿAin Ghazal in Jordanien Kalk mit nicht erhitztem, zerstoßenem Kalkstein zur Herstellung von Gips für die großflächige Verkleidung von Wänden, Böden und Feuerstellen in Häusern. Die alten Ägypter versahen ihre Bauten mit kunstreich bemalten Schichten aus Kalk und Gipsputz. Die Römer verwendeten Kalkputz in Reliefs, um monumentale Architektur nachzuahmen – als erste Kultur, die räumliche Architekturelemente vortäuschte – und diese Praxis wurde von den Architekten der Renaissance wiederbelebt, die geformten Stuck zur Gestaltung von raffinierten Außenornamenten einsetzten.

Die anhaltende Beliebtheit von Stuck ist leicht nachzuvollziehen. Stuck ist billig, widerstandsfähig und kann zu den fantasievollsten Ornamenten geformt werden. Mit Stuck – auch als Stein der armen Leute bezeichnet – lassen sich kostspieligere Baustoffe wie Granit oder Marmor nachahmen, weshalb er an von Steinbrüchen weit entfernten Orten (wie Wien und London) eine breite Verwendung findet.

A RECIPE

To a mixture of lime, water, and sand add:
<u>Blood or cheese</u> to slow down the set of the mixture. For even better results, Gypsum combined with sour milk or wine will enable a slow enough set to allow for the creation of the most intricate of hand modelled ornaments.
<u>Beeswax, fats, or oil</u> will improve water repellency – a highly desirable feature in your new surface
<u>Beer, urine, or whiskey</u> will trap air in the mixture, improving the strength of the set. Sugar will reduce the amount of water needed
<u>Ox, horse, goat, or human hair</u> (at a push) will extend the mixture and give the lime and sand toughness and cohesion.

THE MARBLE OF SUBURBIA – DINGBAT ARCHITECTURE

From the latter half of the 20th century onwards, the most consistent devotees of stucco can be found in the United States. During

Die Rezeptur für Stuck ist flexibel und wurde mit einer Reihe von erstaunlich zufälligen Zutaten gemischt. Im England des 17. Jahrhunderts konnte Putz Obstsaft, Bier, Blut, Käse oder Bienenwachs enthalten – man mischte ihn einfach mit Haushalts- oder Körperflüssigkeiten, um die gewünschte Beschaffenheit zu erreichen.

REZEPTUR

Einer Mischung aus Kalk, Wasser und Sand füge man hinzu:
<u>Blut oder Käse</u>, damit das Gemisch langsamer verfestigt. Für noch bessere Ergebnisse lässt Gips kombiniert mit <u>Sauermilch oder Wein</u> das Gemisch so langsam fest werden, um die feinsten Ornamente von Hand zu formen.
<u>Bienenwachs, Fette und Öl</u> verbessern das Wasserabweisungsvermögen – eine höchst wünschenswerte Eigenschaft für Verputz.
<u>Bier, Urin und Whiskey</u> binden Luft im Gemisch, das damit stärker verfestigt.
<u>Zucker</u> verringert die erforderliche Wasserbeigabe.

the post-war building boom of the 1950s and 60s, despite sneers from Victorian ancestors, stucco was to become a staple of American vernacular architecture. In the West and South West, where brick and stone were expensive and hard to come by, it was to prove a cheap and efficient building material. It found particular favour in California, where, in combination with a lightweight wood framed construction, stucco would stand up to the region's seismic instabilities.

"Stucco is the suburban Carrera marble," writes author D.J. Waldie, in whose first book *Holy Land: A Suburban Memoir* stucco's flimsy membrane coats the architecture of his southern California childhood. "All you need is sand, water, cement and a strong arm and you can turn a stack of sticks and chicken wire into a home."

It was this cheapness and accessibility, rather than the liveliness of its architectural vocabulary that saw stucco embraced across the Atlantic, and a rash of a boxy, rectangular wood and chicken-wire framed stucco buildings spread across the California landscape. Usually two stories worth of bland, plastered exterior wall – like empty pages –

Ochsenhaar, Pferdehaar, Ziegenhaar oder (zur Not) Menschenhaar strecken das Gemisch und verleihen dem Kalk-Sand-Gemisch Festigkeit und Bindekraft.

Der Marmor der Vororte – Dingbat-Architektur

Ab der zweiten Hälfte des 20. Jahrhunderts findet man die treuesten Anhänger des Stucks in den USA. Ungeachtet des Hohns der viktorianischen Vorfahren wurde Stuck im Nachkriegs-Bauboom der 1950er- und 1960er-Jahre zum Grundstein der Architektur der amerikanischen Massen. Im Westen und Südwesten, wo Backstein und Stein teuer und schwer erhältlich waren, erwies er sich als günstiger und tauglicher Baustoff. Besonders beliebt wurde Stuck in Kalifornien, wo er, kombiniert mit leichten Holzrahmenkonstruktionen, auch der Erdbebengefahr der Region standhielt.

„Stuck ist der Carrara-Marmor der Vororte", schrieb der Schriftsteller D. J. Waldie, in dessen Erstlingswerk *Holy Land: A Suburban Memoir* dünne Stuckschichten die Bauten

these buildings, like empty pages, would be adorned with characters.

A dingbat is a typesetting ornament – a special character; a star, tick, arrow, pointing finger. On the page these are tiny. On a Dingbat building, as the California vernacular came to be known, such ornaments are magnified – the points of a stylised star, meters long, the extravagant curves of an atomic symbol, a fantasy lifestyle name in foot high cursive writing. These blank slate buildings are defined by their ornamentation – I'll meet you at Casa Bella, underneath the terracotta starburst.

Coming Entstuckung

While California was embracing exterior ornamentation, parts of Europe were simultaneously rejecting it. In the first half of the 20th century, Berlin and a number of other German cities began a process of un-stuccoing – 'Entstuckung'. Peaking during the post-World War Two period, thousands of buildings and apartment blocks had their facades stripped of ornamental plasterwork.

seiner südkalifornischen Kindheit überziehen. „Man braucht nur Sand, Wasser, Zement und starke Arme, um aus einem Stapel Holz und Maschendraht ein Zuhause zu machen."

Nicht so sehr wegen der Vielfalt an architektonischen Möglichkeiten, sondern weil er erschwinglich war, wurde Stuck auf der anderen Seite des Atlantiks enorm beliebt, und bald überzog eine Flut von kastenförmigen, stuckverputzten Häusern aus Holz- und Drahtrahmenkonstruktion die kalifornische Landschaft. Meist zweistöckig mit blanken, verputzten Außenwänden wurden diese Häuser – wie unbeschriebene Blätter – mit Symbolen, sogenannten Dingbats, verziert.

In der Typografie sind Dingbats Symbole wie etwa Sonderzeichen, Sterne, Häkchen, Pfeile oder Zeiger. Auf einer Druckseite sind sie winzig. Auf einem Dingbat-Haus, wie man die kalifornische Massenarchitektur nannte, wurden diese Ornamente vergrößert – die Spitzen eines stilisierten Sterns wurden meterlang, die Kurven eines Atomsymbols extravagant; erfundene Hausnamen wurden in ellenlanger Kursivschrift angebracht. Diese gesichtslosen Schema-F-Häuser definieren sich über ihre Ornamentik: Wir treffen

The Hauser Apartment
Building, ca. 1958

Where previously buildings had faced the street in imitation of the grandeur of sandstone block construction, or embellished in an eclectic mishmash of architectural styles – baroque, rococo, gothic – they now presented smooth, bare frontages. Unembellished 'honesty' was conquering stuccoed 'deception'. This disrobing of the city began in earnest after 1945. In Berlin's Kreuzberg, for example, more than 1400 buildings had their stucco cut off by 1977.

The movement had its theoretical foundations in the anti-ornamentation stance of early modernists such as Adolf Loos, later taken up by architects of Germany's

uns an der Casa Bella unter dem Terrakotta-Strahlenkranz.

Der Beginn der Entstuckung

Während sich Kalifornien für Ornamente begeisterte, wurden diese in Teilen Europas zeitgleich verworfen. Anfang des 20. Jahrhunderts begann in Berlin und zahlreichen anderen deutschen Städten ein Prozess der Entstuckung, der in der Nachkriegszeit gipfelte, als die Fassaden tausender Gebäude ihres schmückenden Verputzes entkleidet wurden. Während die Bauten zuvor die

Pracht der Sandsteinblockbauweise nachgeahmt oder Verzierungen in einer eklektischen Mischung aus Baustilen – Barock, Rokoko, Gotik – zur Schau gestellt hatten, präsentierten sie jetzt glatte, nackte Fassaden. Die schmucklose „Ehrlichkeit" triumphierte über die verputzte „Täuschung". In Berlin Kreuzberg etwa wurden bis 1977 mehr als 1.400 Gebäude entstuckt.

Ausgehend von der Ablehnung des Ornaments durch Vertreter der frühen Moderne wie Adolf Loos, propagierten die Architekt*innen der Neuen Sachlichkeit in Deutschland klare Linien und funktionale Entwürfe anstelle unnötiger Ausschmückung. Stuck an Mietshäusern wurde nicht nur in architektonischer Hinsicht als unaufrichtig empfunden, er war als Verschleierung von elenden gesellschaftlichen Verhältnissen verpönt: Die prächtigen, schmückenden Fassaden verbargen triste, beengte Innenräume.

Die Architekturgeschichte wimmelt von moralischen Ansprüchen und die Moderne neigte besonders dazu, Baustoffe mit moralischen Urteilen zu versehen. Louis Kahn huldigte dem Backstein, während Mies van

Entstuckung, Prenzlauer Berg, Berlin, 2009, © wikimedia commons_Hhs

New Objectivity Movement, who promoted clean lines and functional designs over unnecessary decoration. The stucco in tenement houses was seen as a falsehood on more than an architectural level – it was considered a veiling of miserable social conditions: the grand, decorative facades hiding cheerless, cramped interiors.

Moral claims populate architectural history, with modernism being a particularly ripe time for attaching moral judgement to materials. Louis Kahn honoured bricks, whilst Mies van der Rohe praised the transparency of glass architecture. Our American visitor to Vienna, Mr Pettit, was perhaps aligning himself with earlier rejections of material 'deception' from within the Arts and Crafts movement and the writings of John Ruskin, whose *Seven Lamps of Architecture* included 'truth': a call for the honest display of materials and structure.

Facades in particular are often discussed using a moral vocabulary – we speak of honesty, truth, purity, dishonesty, falsehood, deception, and fakery. "'The whited sephulchre', the biblical metaphor for a suave surface concealing unspecified corruption, is per-

der Rohe die Transparenz der Glasarchitektur pries. Womöglich sympathisierte Henry Pettit, der amerikanische Besucher in Wien, mit der frühen Ablehnung der stofflichen „Täuschung" durch die Arts-and-Crafts-Bewegung und den Schriften von John Ruskin, zu dessen „sieben Leuchtern der Baukunst" auch die „Wahrheit" gehörte, ein Appell zur wahrhaftigen Darbietung von Stoffen und Strukturen.

Vor allem Fassaden werden oft mit moralischen Begriffen beschrieben – man spricht von Ehrlichkeit, Wahrheit, Reinheit, Unehrlichkeit, Falschheit, Täuschung und Schwindel. „Das ‚getünchte Grabmahl', die biblische Metapher für eine glatte Oberfläche, die eine nebulöse Verderbtheit verbirgt, ist vielleicht die früheste Verunglimpfung", schreibt John Chase in seinem Überblick des südkalifornischen Stadtbildes, *Glitter Stucco and Dumpster Diving*. „Es gibt die unlogische, aber scheinbar tief sitzende Meinung, dass Stuck, da er ein ausschließliches Oberflächenmaterial ist, wohl etwas Ungesundes oder Unsittliches verdeckt."

Die Entstuckung hat in Berlin bleibende Spuren hinterlassen. Wohnblöcke, die bei

Vienna's Wienerberger brickworks at the beginnig of the 19th century
Wienerberger Ziegelproduktion Anfang des 19. Jahrhunderts am Wienerberg,
© Wienerberger

haps the earliest slur" writes John Chase in his tour of the Southern Californian Cityscape: Glitter Stucco and Dumpster Diving. "There is the illogical but apparently ineradicable attitude that since stucco is purely a surface material, what it covers must be unhealthy or immoral."

"Entstuckung" has left a lasting mark on Berlin. Apartment blocks which a casual passer by might assume to have been built in the 1950s may actually be 19th century constructions. In stripping the city of its outer layer, buildings have been de-contextualised, their defining historical and aesthetic characteristics erased – one of the

flüchtigem Blick aus den 1950er-Jahren zu stammen scheinen, sind womöglich aus dem 19. Jahrhundert. Durch das Abtragen der äußeren Schicht wurden die Gebäude aus dem Zusammenhang gerissen, ihre bezeichnenden historischen und ästhetischen Merkmale ausradiert – so lautete der schwerwiegende Vorwurf jener, die das Projekt Ende der 1970er-Jahre schließlich stoppten. Die Vorläufer der Dingbats aus dem 19. Jahrhundert wurden im Interesse der Lauterkeit abgetragen und hinterließen – welch Ironie – dann doch Gebäude, die der Welt weiterhin eine täuschende Fassade präsentieren.

Wienerberger brick storage
Wienerberger Ziegellager,
Hennersdorf, 2016

biggest criticisms of those who eventually halted the project in the late 1970s. The 19th century equivalent of dingbats removed in favour of blankness, leaving buildings that, ironically, continue to present a misleading face to the world.

The stucco paradox

The European pond turtle frolics (if turtles can frolic) in Vienna's ex-claypits, a landscape of parkland and skyscrapers, which bears no traces of the muddy squalor of its clay mining past. Vienna's Wienerberger brickworks have migrated southwards, beyond the city limits, to Hennersdorf, as clay deposits in Wienerberg were exhausted. Where once the brickworks were explicitly tied to the city, they are now detached and out of sight – a metaphor, perhaps, for our own increasing removal from an understanding of the materials which make up our built environment.

In talking about how we build, and about how we communicate how we build, instead of relying on the moral framework, which

Das Stuck-Paradox

Die Europäische Sumpfschildkröte tummelt sich (wenn Schildkröten sich denn tummeln können) in den alten Wiener Lehmgruben, einer Landschaft mit Parks und Hochhäusern, die keine Spuren der Verschmutzung und des Elends im früheren Lehmabbau mehr erkennen lassen. Nachdem die Lehmvorkommen am Wienerberg erschöpft waren, wanderte die Produktion nach Süden ab, über die Stadtgrenze nach Hennersdorf. Während die Ziegelwerke früher deutlich mit der Stadt verbunden waren, sind sie jetzt aus dem Blickfeld verschwunden – vielleicht ein Sinnbild der zunehmenden Entfremdung von jeglichem Verständnis der Baustoffe, aus denen unsere gebaute Umwelt besteht.

Wenn wir darüber sprechen, wie wir bauen und wie wir über das Bauen kommunizieren, sollten wir uns vielleicht das Stuck-Paradox vor Augen halten, anstatt uns auf das Moralgebäude rund um die Frage der Materialgerechtigkeit zu stützen. Stuck dient zwar auch zum Verdecken der tatsächlichen Bausubstanz, ist dafür aber

surrounds the question of material honesty, perhaps we need to consider the stucco paradox. Stucco is at once an agent of mystery – a cover up of the true fabric of a building, and a material of accessibility, an everyman's chicken-wire and sticks construction solution, a flexible shape shifting substance that enables new forms. It is both sham and a medium for easy creativity.

Niamh Riordan is an artist and writer, living in Liverpool, UK. She has written and edited a number of publications alongside Assemble, including the Granby Workshop Catalogue (2015) and A Factory as it Might Be (2017). Her short stories appear in FEAST Magazine (2016), and the forthcoming The Devil's Supper, a publication by the Anthony Burgess Foundation. Niamh is part of Fairland Collective, a group of artists and other professionals who produce projects which build upon the idea of arts being useful in the everyday. Recent projects include One Pot Project (ongoing) with Sefton Libraries (UK) and A Dream for Shimoneseki with Grizedale Arts and Kiwanosato Gathering Group (Japan).

---

ein höchst erschwinglicher Baustoff: eine Lösung für jedermann und jede Konstruktion; ein anpassungsfähiger, gestaltwandelnder Stoff, der neue Formen ermöglicht. Stuck ist sowohl Schein als auch Stoff für schlichte Schöpfungskraft.

Niamh Riordan lebt als Künstlerin und Schriftstellerin in Liverpool (GB). Sie hat für Assemble zahlreiche Publikationen verfasst, darunter den „Granby Workshop Catalogue" (2015) und „A Factory as it Might Be" (2017). Ihre Kurzgeschichten sind im FEAST Magazine (2016) und im „The Devil's Supper" der Anthony Burgess Foundation zu lesen. Sie ist Mitglied von Fairland Collective, einem Kollektiv von Kunstschaffenden, deren Projekte auf dem Gedanken der Nützlichkeit der Künste im Alltag gründen. Zu den jüngsten Projekten gehören „One Pot Project" (laufend) in Zusammenarbeit mit Sefton Libraries (GB) und „A Dream for Shimoneseki" mit Grizedale Arts und Kiwanosato Gathering Group (Japan).

Clay models for the pavilion in the courtyard
of the Architekturzentrum Wien
Ton-Modelle für den Pavillon im Hof
des Architekturzentrum Wien

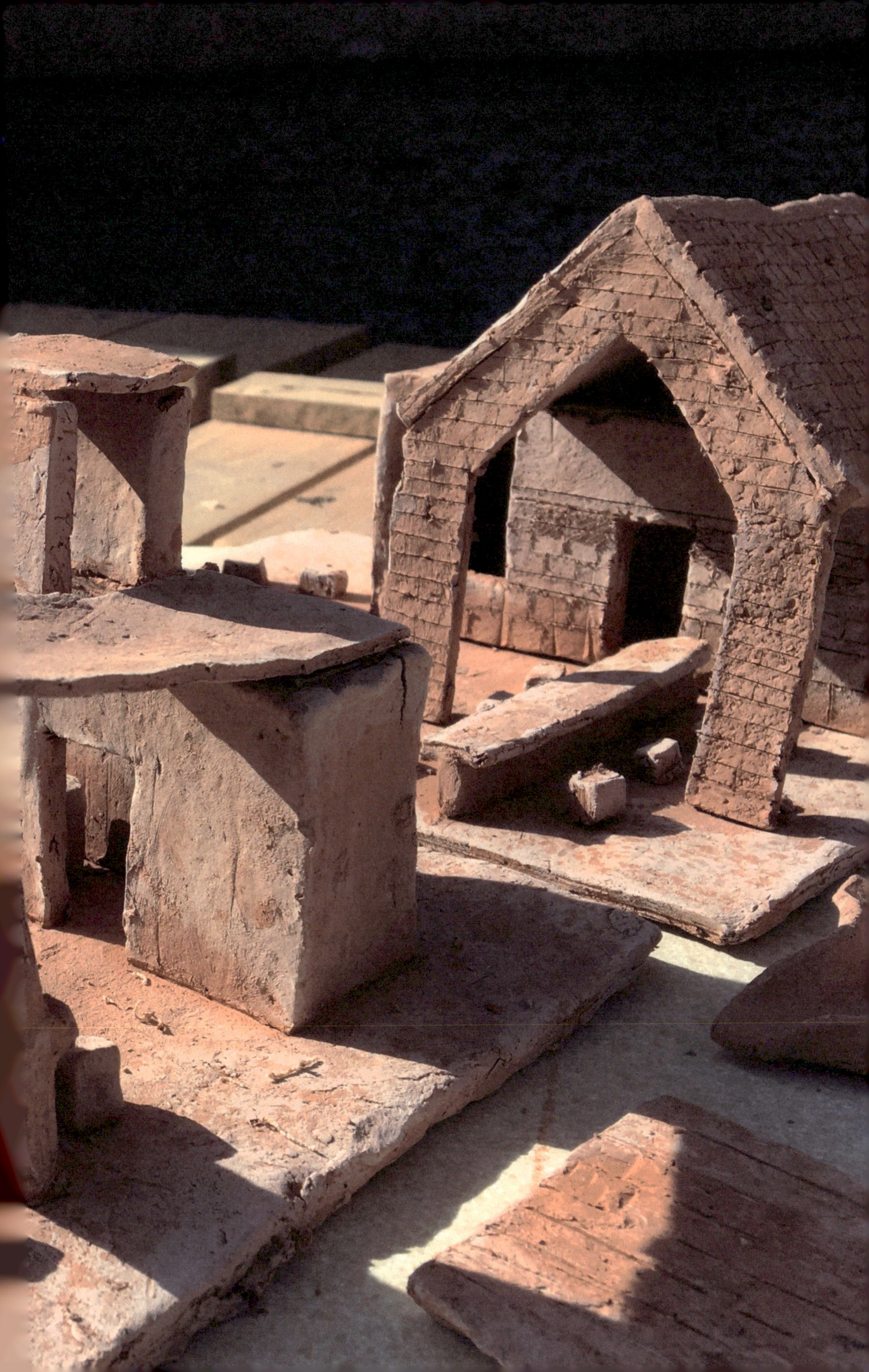

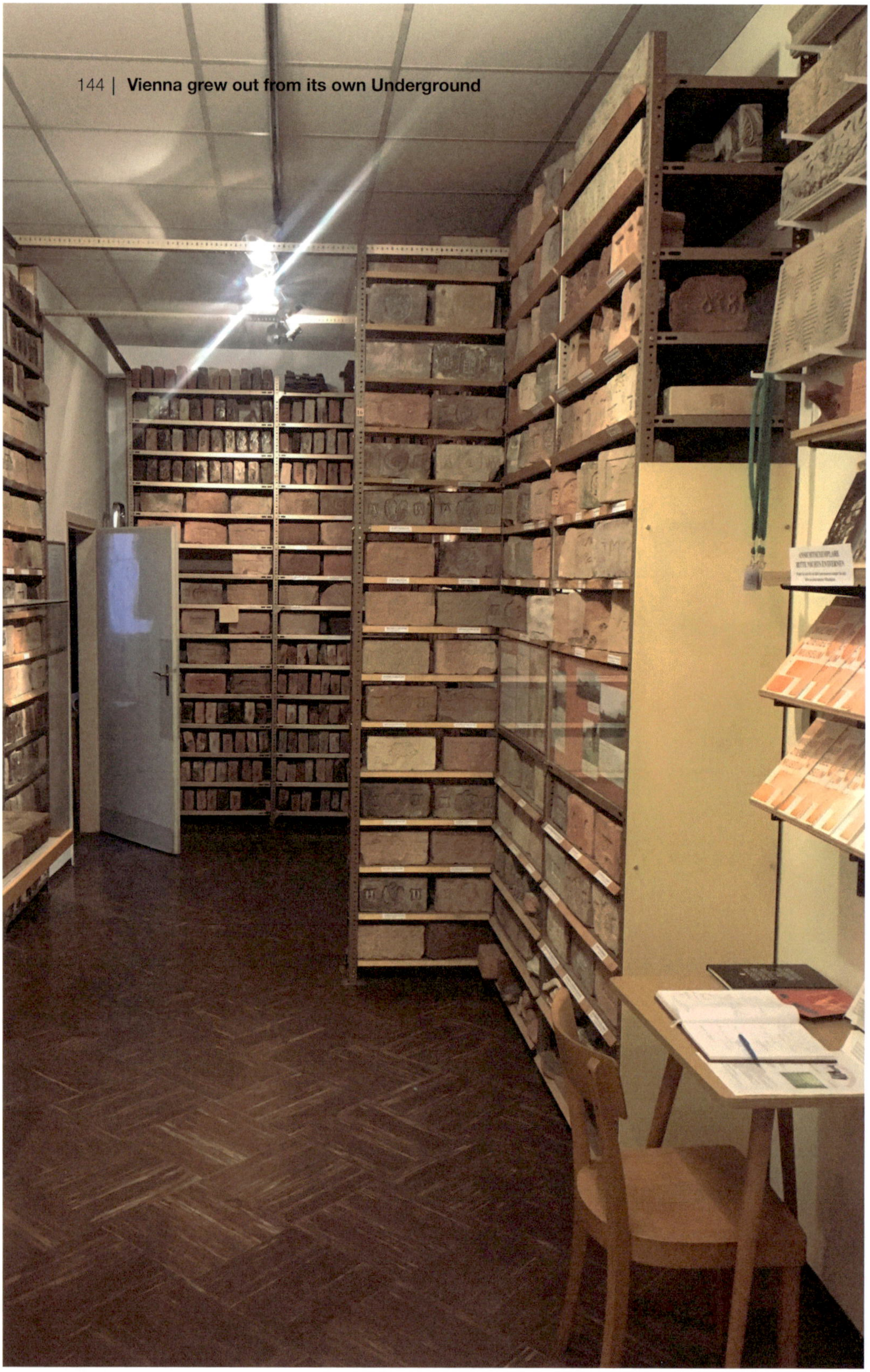

Vienna grew out from its own Underground

Wien ist aus seinem eigenen Untergrund herausgewachsen

"The competition is in full swing: glass vs. brick, steel vs. concrete, airy vs. massive, provocation vs. tradition", ran the headline of the July 1994 edition of the German architecture magazine *Bauwelt*. The article inside went one step further: "Whoever still uses brick today, in the face of high-tech steel-glass facades, will easily be taken for an anachronistic fossil, someone who will go for cosiness rather than using 'modern' materials. There is probably something to it. [...] Brick has gone out of fashion as a facade material, and manufacturers and buyers are equally to blame." Indeed, the predilection for brickwork has swung to and fro from one century to another.

„Der Wettstreit ist voll entbrannt: Glas gegen Ziegel, Stahl gegen Beton, Luftiges gegen Masse, Provokation gegen Tradition", so titelte die Juli-Ausgabe der deutschen Architekturzeitschrift *Bauwelt* im Jahr 1994. Im Heftinneren wird noch nachgelegt: „Wer heute, angesichts hochgezüchteter Stahl-Glas-Fassaden, immer noch Ziegel verwendet, gerät leicht in den Ruf, ein Ewig-Gestriger zu sein, einer, der eher dem Gemüt huldigt, als sich ‚moderner' Mittel zu bedienen. Wohl nicht ganz zu Unrecht. [...] Der Ziegel als Fassadenmaterial ist ziemlich heruntergekommen, und daran sind Hersteller wie Abnehmer gleichermaßen beteiligt."

View into the Wiener Ziegelmuseum
Blick ins Wiener Ziegelmuseum

In the context of their visiting professorship at the Vienna University of Technology, Assemble started the winter semester 2016 by investigating the materiality of Vienna with the students. It was their objective to dissect the physical construction of the city – its skin and bones – and to explore how these methods and materials are a reflection of economic, political, and social conditions. Brick quickly became the focus of their research and the students delved into Vienna's history of construction, and, thus, its specific social and migration history. The summer semester 2017 is dedicated to brick as a modern building material that can be locally produced all over the world and has a wide variety of uses. As a logical conclusion to their research, the students will take a hands-on approach and build a brick pavilion in the courtyard of Architekturzentrum Wien. In a conversation with the head of the unique brick museum in Vienna's 14th District, Gerhard Zsutty, we tried to get to the bottom of this material that like no other marks the cityscape of Vienna.

Our interview partner: Dr. Gerhard Zsutty, born in Vienna in 1939. After graduating in palaeontology and geology he free-lanced

Tatsächlich ist die Akzeptanz von Mauerwerk über die Jahrhunderte immer wieder großen Schwankungen ausgesetzt gewesen.

Im Zuge ihrer Gastprofessur an der TU Wien haben sich Assemble mit den Studierenden gleich zu Beginn des Wintersemesters 2016 mit der Stofflichkeit von Wien auseinandergesetzt. Ziel war es, die physische Struktur der Stadt – sozusagen ihre Knochen und Haut – zu erheben und aus der Analyse der Baumethoden und Materialien auch die wirtschaftlichen, politischen und sozialen Bedingungen zu reflektieren. Schnell stand der Ziegel im Fokus ihrer Forschung und die Studierenden tauchten intensiv in die Baugeschichte Wiens und damit einhergehend in die spezifische Sozial- und Migrationsgeschichte ein. Das Sommersemester 2017 widmet sich nun dem Ziegel als modernem Baumaterial, weltweit regional herstellbar und vielseitig einsetzbar. Als logische Folge der Recherchen errichten die Studierenden als Selbstbauprojekt im Hof des Architekturzentrum Wien einen Pavillon aus Ziegeln.

In einem Gespräch mit dem Direktor des einzigartigen Ziegelmuseums in Wien 14, Gerhard Zsutty, versuchten wir, jenem Ma-

in Portugal for 16 years. Returning to Vienna in 1979, he became a scientific staff member of the Wiener Ziegelmuseum, an offshoot of the Penzing District Museum. Upon reaching retirement, he became scientific head of the museum and remains intimately engaged in brick research.

Az W Brick is a very important building material in many countries, but not always in the form of exposed brickwork, as we know it from northern Germany, the UK, or the Netherlands, where Brick Expressionism spawned a great number of brick-faced structures. Why was exposed brickwork never a big issue in Vienna? Or was it indeed at some point, and then it just disappeared?
Zsutty: For a short time it actually was an issue, for instance with Ludwig Förster and Theophil Hansen. Both wanted to propagate this type of construction and a few clinker facades were built, but unfortunately it was not a lasting trend. One of the reasons is certainly that there is very little suitable clay for that type of clinker in Austria. Some, but not very much, is to be found along the River Danube, in Schwertberg and Pöchlarn, for instance,

terial ein wenig auf den Grund zu gehen, das die Stadt Wien maßgeblich prägt.

Unser Gesprächspartner ist Dr. Gerhard Zsutty, geboren 1939 in Wien, der nach dem Studium der Paläontologie und der Geologie während eines 16-jährigen Aufenthaltes in Portugal freiberuflich tätig war. Im Jahr 1979 folgte die Rückkehr nach Wien, wo er als wissenschaftlicher Mitarbeiter im Wiener Ziegelmuseum, einer Außenstelle des Bezirksmuseums Penzing, arbeitete. Seit der Pensionierung ist er wissenschaftlicher Leiter des Museums und intensiv mit der Ziegelforschung befasst.

Az W: Der Ziegel hat in vielen Ländern als Baumaterial große Bedeutung, aber nicht überall ist er als Sichtziegel ausgeführt, wie man das etwa aus Norddeutschland, Großbritannien oder den Niederlanden kennt, wo im Zuge des Ziegelexpressionismus sehr viele Sichtziegelbauten entstanden sind. Warum war das sichtbar bleibende Mauerwerk in Wien eigentlich nie ein Thema? Oder war es eines und ist wieder verschwunden?
Zsutty: Es war kurze Zeit auch hier ein Thema, etwa bei Ludwig Förster und Theophil

which can withstand temperatures of up to 1200 degrees. A normal clay brick cannot take such high temperatures. In northern Germany or England, you will find clays that withstand much higher temperatures. There, they developed a double-layer construction method – with backing bricks made from regular clay and clinker bricks for the facing layer.

Az W: So, it's not so much for aesthetic reasons that they immediately plaster everything over hereabouts?

Zsutty: People preferred to plaster over handmade bricks – particularly if they were made or laid shoddily – because they didn't look very nice. So the plaster served to hide the inept workmanship. Theophil Hansen, for one, always complained loudly about brickwork being covered up so ashamedly although it was such a beautiful material. Alois Miesbach, the owner of nine large brick-making factories employing 4,700 workers, which made him the continent's biggest brick tycoon in the mid-19th century [editor's note], developed a double elutriation process resulting in a brick of much heavier weight and density. It was

Hansen. Beide propagierten diese Art des Bauens und ein paar Backsteinbauten sind auch entstanden, aber leider wurde das nicht weiterverfolgt. Ein Grund dafür ist sicher, dass der für die Herstellung dieser Art von Klinker notwendige Ton in Österreich kaum vorkommt. Lediglich entlang der Donau, etwa in Schwertberg und in Pöchlarn, gibt es welchen, der Temperaturen bis 1.200 Grad verträgt. Ein normaler Mauerziegel hält so hohen Temperaturen nicht stand. In Norddeutschland oder zum Beispiel in England gibt es Tone, die wesentlich höhere Temperaturen vertragen. Dort hat man eine Zweischalenbauweise entwickelt: den Hintermauerziegel aus normalem Ton mit der vorgesetzten Klinkerfassade.

Az W: Es sind also weniger ästhetische Gründe, dass bei uns alles sofort verputzt wird?

Zsutty: Die handgemachten Ziegel – vor allem wenn sie schlampig hergestellt oder vermauert wurden – hat man lieber verputzt, weil sie kein schöner Anblick waren. Der Verputz diente also dazu, die Sünden zu verstecken. Theophil Hansen hat sich aber immer darüber beschwert, dass der Ziegel, der ja ein schönes Material ist, schamhaft

Wien ist aus seinem eigenen Untergrund herausgewachsen | 149

Gerhard Zsutty, Director
of the Wiener Ziegelmuseum
Gerhard Zsutty, Leiter des Wiener
Ziegelmuseums © Sonja Pisarik

produced in a mould, but then compacted again in a manual press, which resulted in very sharp and exact edges. In order to distinguish these special bricks from regular bricks, the usual maker's mark was stamped on them perpendicularly rather than horizontally. With that brick you could produce very nice exposed brickwork facades. But a much greater effort was involved in their production, of course.

AzW: Would you say that Vienna's situation is very specific when it comes to brickmaking or the use of brick?

Zsutty: Vienna had the wonderful advantage of being able to grow out from its own underground. A good part of the subsoil in Vienna consists of high-quality marine clay. You just need to remove the glacial Danubian gravel layer, normally two, but never more than three metres thick, and you have this wonderful clay. Brick construction is the natural way to go in such a case.

AzW: But isn't it generally true that wherever people used brick for building, the bricks were produced locally?

Zsutty: There was a very interesting phenomenon in northern Germany. The Ro-

versteckt wird. Alois Miesbach, der in der Mitte des 19. Jahrhunderts als Besitzer von neun großen Ziegeleien mit insgesamt 4.700 Beschäftigten größter Ziegelhersteller des Kontinents war *[Anm. d. Red.]*, entwickelte einen doppelt geschlämmten Ziegel. Dieser war wesentlich schwerer und dichter. Er wurde zwar auch in einem Model gemacht, aber dann mit einer handbetätigten Presse nachgepresst, so wurde er schön scharfkantig und exakt. Um diese speziellen Ziegel gut von den normalen Mauerziegeln zu unterscheiden, wurde das übliche Ziegelzeichen nicht querformatig, sondern hochkant angebracht. Mit so einem Ziegel konnte man sehr schöne Sichtziegelfassaden machen. Aber das war natürlich viel aufwendiger.

AzW: Würden Sie sagen, dass die Wiener Situation eine sehr spezifische ist, was die Ziegelerzeugung oder auch die Verwendung von Ziegeln betrifft?

Zsutty: Wien hatte den wunderbaren Vorteil, dass es regelrecht aus seinem eigenen Untergrund herauswachsen konnte, der aus einem guten Meeres-Ton besteht. Man muss nur die eiszeitlichen Schichten Donauschotter wegräumen, das sind meistens zwei, ma-

manesque buildings there are all still built of stones. Until the 12th century, the builders used boulders deposited there by glacial moraines. Once that resource was exhausted, they had to use clay, which was also found there. Loam, loess, and clay are actually products of weathering you will find everywhere. I know some interesting churches from the Romanesque period which are made of stone up to a certain height and then the walls suddenly continue as brickwork, because the builders ran out of stone.

AzW: Brick also has a long tradition as a "poor man's" building material, or, to phrase that differently: its popularity decreased in the 20th century through industrialisation and the advent of concrete. Whilst Vienna was

ximal drei Meter, und dann kommt schon der wunderbare Ton zutage. Damit bietet sich der Ziegelbau natürlich sehr an.

AzW: Aber ist nicht überall dort, wo mit Ziegeln gebaut wurde, der Ziegel ein regionales Produkt gewesen?

Zsutty: In Norddeutschland konnte man ein sehr interessantes Phänomen beobachten: Die romanischen Bauten sind alle noch aus Feldsteinen erbaut. Man hat bis ins 12. Jahrhundert Findlinge verwendet, die von den Moränen zurückgelassen wurden. Irgendwann war diese Ressource erschöpft und man musste zum Ton übergehen, der ja auch dort abgelagert war. Lehm, Ton und Löss finden sich eigentlich überall als Verwitterungsprodukte. Ich kenne einige interessante Kirchen aus der Romanik, die bis in eine gewisse Höhe aus Stein gebaut sind und dann in Ziegelmauerwerk übergehen, weil keine Steine mehr vorhanden waren.

AzW: Der Ziegel hat ja auch eine lange Tradition als „armes" Baumaterial, oder sagen wir so: Das gute Image wurde im 20. Jahrhundert durch die Industrialisierung und das Aufkommen von Beton zurückgedrängt. Nachdem in Wien der Ziegel lange Zeit eine

Construction model for the pavilion in the courtyard of the AzW
Konstruktionsmodell für den Pavillon im Hof des AzW

largely built on brick in days gone by, brick tended later to lose ground.

Zsutty: I can't really understand that, because as it turns out, brick is much more durable than anything else. If you look at how concrete structures age, how quickly they become dilapidated and how long a brick structure survives…

AzW: There is a sense of brick construction experiencing a kind of revival in the last 15 years. After a period of experimenting with other materials it has been found that the old brick masonry has its qualities after all…

Zsutty: … qualities no other material has. What is to be done now with all these fancy concrete buildings, on top of which they slap that pointless Styrofoam?

AzW: Well – I guess the Styrofoam would harm brickwork as well.

Zsutty: Alas it would, unfortunately! But as long as that lobby exists there is nothing one can do, because everybody believes in it.

AzW: But isn't brick getting a certain boost now that sustainability and ecology are important issues?

Zsutty: I for one haven't noticed that, seeing as there is still no getting away from pre-fab

große Bedeutung hatte, ist man davon dann ein wenig weggekommen.

Zsutty: Ja, und ich kann das nicht wirklich nachvollziehen, denn es hat sich herausgestellt, dass der Ziegel wesentlich haltbarer ist als alles andere. Man muss sich ja nur ansehen, wie die Betonbauwerke altern, wie schnell sie kaputt sind und wie lange im Vergleich dazu der Ziegelbau steht.

AzW: Man hat aber das Gefühl, dass der Ziegelbau in den letzten 15 Jahren eine Art Revival erlebt. Nach einer Zeit der Experimente mit anderen Materialien zeigt sich, dass die alte Ziegelmauer Qualitäten aufweist …

Zsutty: … die kein anderes Material besitzt. Was soll man denn mit den Betonbauten machen, denen dann auch noch das unsinnige Styropor draufgeklatscht wird?

AzW: Wobei – Styropor würde wohl auch den Ziegelbau kaputt machen.

Zsutty: Ja, leider! Aber gegen diese Lobby ist man machtlos, weil jeder daran glaubt.

AzW: Der Ziegel erhält aber in Zeiten der Nachhaltigkeit und der Ökologie wieder einen gewissen Aufwind, oder?

Zsutty: Bislang konnte ich das leider so nicht beobachten, weil man ja noch immer nicht

concrete elements. But I am convinced that brick is going to develop further.

AzW: I suppose it is going to remain more expensive, because the amount of work entailed at the construction site is different from concrete.

Zsutty: Well, the first courses of bricks need to be laid very precisely, but then work can progress quite quickly, because bricks are only joined together using polyurethane adhesive nowadays.

AzW: What made you become so extraordinarily interested in brick?

Zsutty: Long story! I first came into contact with bricks as a little boy, because the postwar bomb sites in Vienna were an ideal playground. And when you crawl around in the rubble you find that these bricks all bear makers' marks. I have always been a collector and very systematic, and I quickly saw that there were differing brick marks. That's how I started to collect bricks. Since we had no furniture left, as everything had been destroyed or stolen, I built shelves for my toys and school things with the bricks and boards I found. Later, we got furniture again, the bricks disappeared into the

von diesen Betonfertigteilen wegkommt, aber ich bin überzeugt, der Ziegel wird sich weiterentwickeln.

AzW: Er wird aber immer teurer bleiben, weil die Verarbeitung auf der Baustelle eine andere ist als beim Beton.

Zsutty: Naja, die ersten Reihen der Planziegel müssen sehr genau gearbeitet sein, aber dann geht es sehr flott voran, weil ja die Ziegel nur noch mittels Polyurethan-Kleber aneinandergefügt werden.

AzW: Woher kommt eigentlich Ihr außergewöhnliches Interesse am Ziegel?

Zsutty: Das ist ein lange Geschichte! Meinen ersten Kontakt mit Ziegeln hatte ich als kleiner Bub, weil ich in den Kriegsruinen von Wien das ideale Spielterrain gefunden hatte. Beim Herumkriechen in den Ruinen habe ich festgestellt, dass alle Ziegel Zeichen haben. Ich war immer ein Sammler und systematisch veranlagt und habe schnell gesehen, dass es verschiedene Ziegelzeichen gibt. So habe ich damit begonnen, Ziegel zu sammeln. Da wir keine Möbel mehr hatten, weil alles kaputt oder gestohlen war, habe ich mir für meine Spiel- und Schulsachen aus den gefundenen Ziegeln und Brettern eine Stel-

basement, and I forgot about them. I didn't think of them for a long time, but my mother kept them in the basement, for you never know… After graduating from university I spent 16 years abroad and when I came back they had just reopened the brick museum. I cleared up the basement and found those bricks. And then I suddenly got interested in where these bricks came from and what the marks meant. I copied the marks and came here to the museum to meet the director at that time. He was able to tell me something about some of the bricks, but not about all of them. So I thought: what sort of a museum is this? I come here with my little collection of bricks and they can't tell me anything about them… but I was told that they were urgently looking for someone to do some basic research, because that had never been done. After thinking about it for three days I said: "Ok, I'll do it." Initially I just helped out a little once a week, then it got more, and now it's a full-time job.

AzW: How long have you been working here?
Zsutty: Since 1979! And since the mid-1980s it has become very intensive…
AzW: It is a large museum, after all.

lage gebaut. Später kamen wieder Möbel ins Haus und die Ziegel verschwanden im Keller und damit auch aus meinem Gedächtnis. Ich habe dann lange nicht mehr an sie gedacht, aber meine Mutter hat sie im Keller aufgehoben, weil man weiß ja nie … Nach dem Studium war ich 16 Jahre lang im Ausland, und bei meiner Rückkehr hatte gerade das Ziegelmuseum neu eröffnet. Ich habe den Keller aufgeräumt und bin auf diese Ziegel gestoßen. Und plötzlich war mein Interesse geweckt, woher diese Ziegel kommen und was die Zeichen bedeuten. Ich habe sie also abgezeichnet und bin hierher ins Museum zum damaligen Leiter gegangen. Der konnte mir zu einigen etwas sagen, zu anderen nicht. Ich habe mir gedacht: Was ist denn das für ein Museum? Ich komme mit ein paar Ziegeln und die können mir nichts dazu sagen … Mir wurde aber mitgeteilt, dass dringend jemand zur Grundlagenforschung gesucht werde, weil das noch nie geschehen sei. Nach drei Tagen Bedenkzeit habe ich gesagt: „Ich mache es." Auf diese Weise habe ich zuerst einmal pro Woche ein bisschen mitgeholfen, dann sukzessive mehr und jetzt ist es ein Fulltime-Job.

Various bricks – collection
of the Wiener Ziegelmuseum
Ziegel aus der Sammlung des
Wiener Ziegelmuseums

Zsutty: Yes, but I need more space! I would like to put much more on display – there are many goodies just lying in storage!
AzW: I don't think there is really a single museum on earth that wouldn't like to have more space. Your museum is also closely connected to the history of a city, namely Vienna.
Zsutty: True, but I don't collect bricks only from Austria, of course, but from beyond the confines of the former Hapsburg monarchy, from all over Europe and worldwide. Since I have travelled quite a bit I have brought back many things with me from everywhere I've been. And there are more and more people collecting, I'm sorry to say! That means we ourselves miss out on many good things. In older buildings there are often interesting

AzW: Wie lange sind Sie schon hier tätig?
Zsutty: Seit 1979! Und seit Mitte der 1980er-Jahre eben sehr intensiv.
AzW: Es ist ja auch ein großes Museum.
Zsutty: Ja, aber ich brauche mehr Platz! Ich hätte gerne viel mehr ausgestellt – da gäbe es noch so einiges im Depot!
AzW: Es gibt, glaube ich, kein Museum auf der ganzen Welt, dass nicht gerne mehr Platz hätte. Ihr Museum hat auch viel mit der Geschichte der Stadt Wien zu tun.
Zsutty: Ja, aber ich sammle natürlich nicht nur Ziegel aus Österreich, sondern über die ehemalige Monarchie hinausgehend, aus ganz Europa und weltweit. Ich bin ja viel in der Welt herumgekommen und habe von überall her etwas mitgebracht. Es gibt mittlerweile – sehr zu meinem Leidwesen – auch immer mehr Sammler, wodurch uns natürlich einiges entgeht. In älteren Häusern existieren immer interessante Stücke, die einfach verschwinden. Wenn ich etwas von einem Abriss oder einer Baustelle höre, gehe ich sofort hin, aber oft ist die Hälfte des Hauses schon weg. Ich habe immer geweint, wenn ich in den 1960er-Jahren gesehen habe, dass irgendwo ein Gerüst aufgebaut

pieces and they just disappear, if I'm too late. Whenever I hear of a demolition or a building site in the offing, I go there immediately, but often half of the old structure is already gone. It made me cry, in the 1960s, every time I saw scaffolding going up somewhere. I knew then: that facade has been lost. They just brutally wrecked everything – really bad. In the 1960s, Vienna lost more than it did during the war! There are districts where the facades of entire streets have gone.

Az W: That's true! But in the late 1960s, early 1970s, an awareness grew of the value of old building stock.

Zsutty: Too late, in many cases! And it's continuing. There are still beautiful old buildings from the late 19th century that are being torn down!

Az W: Assemble also came to see your museum. They plan to build a brick pavilion in our courtyard at the Architekturzentrum Wien with students of architecture. A few weeks ago they had the first design class and the students were very eager to design a true and genuine brick structure.

Zsutty: I think it's wonderful that the students are exploring their city and the material it is

wird. Denn da wusste ich gleich: Diese Fassade ist verloren. Es wurde einfach brutal alles abgeschlagen – ganz schlimm. Wien hat in den 1960er-Jahren mehr verloren als im Krieg! Es gibt Bezirke, in denen reihenweise ganze Straßenfassaden weg sind.

Az W: Stimmt! Aber Ende der 1960er- und Anfang der 1970er-Jahre hat dann ein Bewusstsein für alte Bausubstanz eingesetzt.

Zsutty: Aber in vielen Fällen zu spät! Und das setzt sich bis heute fort. Immer noch werden schöne alte Gründerzeitbauten abgerissen!

Az W: Assemble waren ja auch hier bei Ihnen im Museum. Sie haben vor, mit Studierenden der TU Wien bei uns im Hof des Architekturzentrum Wien einen Pavillon aus Ziegeln zu bauen. Vor ein paar Wochen gab es das erste Entwerfen und die Studierenden haben den großen Ehrgeiz entwickelt, einen waschechten Ziegelbau zu errichten.

Zsutty: Ich finde es wunderbar, dass sich die Studierenden mit ihrer Stadt und dem Material, aus dem sie gebaut wurde, auseinandersetzen. Durch ihre Analysen wird ja auch ein Stück Sozialgeschichte der Stadt freigelegt. Und vielleicht verhilft die intensive Beschäftigung, die in ein reales Bauwerk – den

built from. Their analyses also reveal a piece of the city's social history. And perhaps this effort, which translates into a real-life building – the Az w pavilion – will help to give brick greater public appeal? Speaking of which: Servus TV produced a series on Emperor Franz Joseph and the Ringstrasse era. The film team contacted me and sent along a few actors who came dressed up as 19th century brick workers from Bohemia. I showed them how manual brickmaking worked at the time and, of course, I thought they wouldn't be able to handle that. But: they made three bricks and the third one was already perfect. The film is really nice, by the way. Television people always like coming to see me. I even had a TV team from China!

Az W: That means your museum is known even in China!

Zsutty: Yes, it's rather well known by now – thank goodness!

INTERVIEW:
SONJA PISARIK,
KATHARINA RITTER

Pavillon fürs Az W – mündet, dem Ziegel zu mehr Öffentlichkeit? Apropos: Servus TV hat eine Serie zu Franz Joseph und der Ringstraßenzeit gedreht. Eine Episode beschäftigt sich auch mit der Frage, wo und wie die Ziegel für die Ringstraße hergestellt wurden. Das Filmteam ist an mich herangetreten und hat mir ein paar Schauspieler geschickt, die verkleidet als Ziegel-Böhmen aufgetaucht sind. Ich habe den Schauspielern gezeigt, wie die händische Ziegelproduktion damals ausgesehen hat und habe mir natürlich gedacht, dass die das nicht zusammenbringen werden. Aber: Drei Ziegel haben sie gemacht und schon der dritte war perfekt. Der Film ist übrigens sehr nett geworden. Das Fernsehen ist immer wieder gerne bei mir. Sogar das chinesische war schon da!

Az W: Das heißt, Ihr Museum kennt man auch in China!

Zsutty: Ja, es ist schon ziemlich bekannt – Gott sei Dank!

INTERVIEW:
SONJA PISARIK,
KATHARINA RITTER

Subventionsgeber / Public funding Az W:

Wien! voraus — Das Zukunftsressort
WIEN KULTUR
BUNDESKANZLERAMT ÖSTERREICH
KUNST

Medienpartner / Media partners:

DER STANDARD
ORF ÖSTERREICH 1 CLUB

Unterstützt von / Supported by:

ARCHITECTURE LOUNGE
Architekturzentrum Wien

Das umfangreiche Programm des Az W wird zu einem beachtlichen Teil von den Beiträgen seines Membership-Programmes und im Besonderen von den Beiträgen seiner Architecture Lounge Partner getragen. In dieser Plattform für engagierte Unternehmen und Verbände wird dem Wissensaustausch und dem Netzwerk-Gedanken oberste Priorität eingeräumt. Learning, Networking und Hospitality sind jene Begriffe, die dieses Kommunikationsfeld zwischen Architektur, Wirtschaft und Politik am besten beschreiben.

A good part of the Az W's comprehensive programme is supported by the contributions from its membership programme, particularly the contributions from its Architecture Lounge partners. This platform for highly committed companies and associations attributes top priority to knowledge exchanges and networking. Learning, networking and hospitality are the notions that best describe this field of communication at the nexus of architecture, business and politics.

aspern Die Seestadt Wiens · BIG · BUWOG group · ERSTE Mehr/WERT Sponsoring · ERSTE Group · eternit

GESIBA · josko FENSTER & TÜREN · Kallco · Mischek · NEUE HEIMAT GEWOG nhg

ÖSW · ÖVW · SOZIALBAU AG Mehr als ein Dach über dem Kopf · storaenso · STRABAG · VIP

vitra · WBV-GPA WOHNBAUVEREINIGUNG FÜR PRIVATANGESTELLTE · WKO WIRTSCHAFTSKAMMER ÖSTERREICH GESCHÄFTSSTELLE BAU · wohnfonds_wien fonds für wohnbau und stadterneuerung · WSE